On Holiday with God

Sue Pickering is an Anglican priest in New Zealand. She has been involved at a national level in the training of spiritual directors and is currently a Canon of Taranaki Cathedral Church, New Plymouth, and chaplain to a retirement community. She is the author of *Creative Ideas for Quiet Days*, *Creative Retreat Ideas* and *Spiritual Direction: A Practical Introduction*, all published by Canterbury Press.

Also by the same author and available from Canterbury Press:

Creative Ideas for Quiet Days: Resources and Liturgies for Retreats and Days of Reflection
With CD Rom
'a veritable feast ... a treasury of ideas and encouragement'
Margaret Silf

Spiritual Direction: A Practical Introduction
'This is quite simply the book on spiritual direction we've been waiting on for years.'
Gordon Jeff

Creative Retreat Ideas: Resources for Short, Day and Weekend Retreats
'An excellent book. Highly recommended.'
The Good Bookstall

www.canterburypress.co.uk

On Holiday with God

Making Your Own Retreat
– A Companion and Guide

Sue Pickering

CANTERBURY
PRESS
Norwich

© Sue Pickering 2012

First published in 2012 by the Canterbury Press Norwich
Editorial office
Invicta House
108–114 Golden Lane,
London, EC1Y OTG, UK

Canterbury Press is an imprint of Hymns Ancient & Modern Ltd
(a registered charity)
13A Hellesdon Park Road, Norwich,
Norfolk, NR6 5DR, UK

www.canterburypress.co.uk

British Library Cataloguing in Publication data

A catalogue record for this book is available
from the British Library

978 1 84825 213 4

Typeset by Regent Typesetting
Printed and bound in Great Britain by
CPI Group (UK) Ltd, Croydon, CRO 4YY

To God who is good
beyond all measure …

and for Gwyneth,
my mother

Contents

Introduction

I took my dog on retreat once.

It was a mistake.

I had chosen to take her for company and security at night, but:
when I wanted to write in my journal, she wanted a walk;
when I wanted to pray, she wanted attention, pushing her moist
   muzzle into my cupped hands;
when I wanted to rest, she wanted to play;
when I wanted to think, she wanted her dinner.

And so it went on.

Much as I loved her and enjoyed her company, it was very clear
that she was a distraction. And distractions, even cuddly ones, get
in the way of the purpose of making a personal retreat – giving
God our *whole* attention, making ourselves available to the Spirit,
so we can begin to glimpse something of the wonder of God's love
for us and be resourced for our encounters with others when we
return home.

In these pages, you'll find some hints on making the most of
retreat time 'on holiday with God' and some suggested themes
from which to choose a focus for all or part of your retreat. As
a 'companion' on your retreat, this little book is not meant to be
a straitjacket, boxing you in with 'oughts' and 'shoulds', but is
designed to support and assist you as you venture into what may
feel like uncharted territory.

Freedom to respond to what God is doing in and with you,
and freedom to choose what fits your personality, health, spiritual
experiences and particular needs, are at the core of retreat time.
Because our God is a God of surprises, you never quite know
what will happen when you go on holiday with God. However,
what you *can* be sure of is that God will honour the effort you are
making to deepen your relationship with God, and you will come
to know yourself more clearly in the process.

List of illustrations

The publisher and author acknowledge with thanks permission to use photographs. Wikimedia Commons images are available under a Creative Commons Attribution-ShareAlike 3.0 licence. Unattributed photographs are by the author.

I

Preparing for your holiday with God

We all know the signs of needing a holiday in the ordinary sense: work and people increasingly sap our energy, Mondays come round too quickly, little things become annoying, and we feel in need of a change, or at least a rest, to recharge our batteries.

But what are the signs of needing a different sort of holiday – a holiday with God? The signs are far more subtle:

- an inner restlessness that's not linked to our outward circumstances
- a persistent wondering about matters of the spirit – faith, forgiveness, suffering, the purpose of our being
- a growing sense that there must be more to life, more to God
- a longing for something we struggle to name.

As we begin to be aware of this yearning, a tiny miracle takes place. Amid the boisterous routines of much of our contemporary life, a personal invitation slips softly into our searching mind, gently insistent. 'Come with me ... to a quiet place and get some rest,' Jesus says (Mark 6.31).

Jesus offered his disciples that invitation two millennia ago. That same invitation has been there in *our* souls since our birth, waiting to surface, waiting for the time when we are still enough, and restless enough, to notice it.

Perhaps picking up this book is the first step you've taken to saying your 'yes' to time apart with God. It may be a tiny, even timid 'yes', but it's coming from somewhere within you that is true and deep and yearning for life in all its fullness – the life that Jesus offers.

Or perhaps you have already begun to respond to Jesus' invitation. You may have attended a quiet day or a mini-retreat, or taken some intentional retreat time at home and been drawn to the slower pace, the time to reflect – and you want more.

Whatever your previous experience, something is drawing you to the 'more' of God, and that something is actually a 'Someone' – the Holy Spirit who has brought to your longing heart this invitation to come on holiday with God, the God who delights in your company, and wants to refresh and renew you.

As with any holiday, it's natural to have a few questions and to gather some information before you make up your mind, so the following sections contain some common questions and some suggestions in response.

How will I find the time?

'You can always find time for the things you want to do,' I can still hear my mother saying! However, we all know that when we are adults with responsibilities, it's not always that easy. There are likely to be competing claims on your time and resources as you listen to the voices of duty and service, and care for those around you. You may even live in an environment where your spiritual life is not supported, or even actively denigrated, and it's a struggle for others to understand your need for time out with God.

But, as you persevere in your desire for the more of God, in spite of the obstacles you may face, the voice of Jesus continues to call you gently, persistently, to spend some time apart with him. At some point, a choice has to be made: either respond to that divine invitation or push it into the background until you are older, have more time, don't have to care for elderly parents, have more money, don't have a noisy two year old ...

There are always going to be a hundred reasons why you cannot go on holiday with God ... but if you sense even as you read this, that you want to go – then tell God of your longing and of any barriers to getting away. Trust the Holy Spirit to work with you to help you make this holiday with God a reality.

How long should my retreat be?

There are no 'rights' and 'wrongs' to the length of a retreat, but you probably know from experience that going away for just a day does not have the same benefits as a lengthier holiday. Similarly, while God will honour your effort to put a day aside, God can do much more with you and for you if you are able to go on holiday with God for a weekend or, even better, for several days. It takes most of us at least one to two days to begin to let go of the busyness and 'on alert' feeling of stress arousal which is a constant reality for many people. It follows that if we are only just beginning to relax after two days on retreat, having another few days with God before we have to return home can be deeply valuable. However, just do what you can manage and leave the rest to God.

What makes a holiday with God different?

When we arrange a holiday, most of us concentrate our planning on what to see, where to stay, and what we can afford. But when we go on holiday with God, we are less concerned by these externals, and more interested in the One with whom we've chosen to spend some time. In fact, a retreat away with God can be compared to going on honeymoon. While the attractions of the honeymoon location are a bonus, all that really matters for newlyweds is to be with their beloved, with no one else around and no other distractions.

You are God's beloved ...

◊ Stop for a moment and let that sink in.

You are responding to that amazing truth by offering God your time and loving attention, choosing not a holiday of busyness and sightseeing, but a 'holyday', in which you open yourself to God as fully as you can. In uncluttered silence, in the sanctuary of solitude, you can discover God's unique way of loving you.

I like the idea of God loving me, but I'm not sure about solitude and silence

For many of us, true solitude is rare. Because our days are often punctuated by conversations and commitments which involve others, the idea of going away and being *on our own* can create uncertainty, even a hint of panic, until we realize that solitude is *not* the same as loneliness. Inevitably this movement into silence, this embracing of solitude with God, will mean an adjustment in your pace, focus, intention and receptivity. Just as pain in child-birth has a redemptive purpose, solitude on retreat helps you give life to your longing for God. This solitude is *for a season*, a planned withdrawal from the myriad distractions of everyday life, so that you can be more attentive to God. Jesus regularly chose such solitude:

> Very early in the morning, while it was still dark,
> Jesus got up, left the house and went off to a
> solitary place, where he prayed.
> (Mark 1.35)

Jesus needed to withdraw from the crowds clamouring for healing so he could spend time with his Father in heart-to-heart prayer, and be resourced for the new day and its demands. If the Son of God took this time apart for his own spiritual health and strengthening, we can do no less.

Solitude's consort is silence, perhaps the most challenging aspect of making a retreat. Many of us live and work in the context of constant man-made noise. *Exterior silence* is hard enough to find in an urban setting, but even in a remote location there will be sound: birdsong, the murmur of streams, the roar of the sea, the wildness or whisper of wind as creation celebrates its life. On retreat it is *interior silence or stillness* which is often a struggle for us, habituated as we are to our interior chatter. Slowing down this personal flow of thoughts is part of the process of settling into our holiday with God, so our mind can be quietly receptive to God's 'still, small voice'.

What about those of us who like talking to other people?

Extraverts among us, those who are energized by people, may have little experience of being on our own and wonder if we can actually gain anything from such a radical change to how we normally find connection with God – in corporate worship and in group contexts. But Scripture is quite clear about the need for solitude and silence, for set-aside times when as *individuals* we are committed to being available *to listen* to God. Psalm 62.5 puts it well:

For God alone my soul waits in silence,
for my hope is from him.

'For God alone' – how beautiful is that intention, that longing to be wholly focused, fully attentive to God. This gladdens God's heart and reminds us of the source of our hopefulness.

No matter whether your natural preference is to process your ideas inwardly or externally, when you go away on retreat you are entering the welcoming warmth of God, as the Spirit calms your interior chatter and opens you up to God's life in you. Choosing this solitude and silence is an act of humility as you acknowledge your poverty and need of God, and a token of trust as you learn to lean more and more on God's goodness.

Isn't going away on retreat selfish?

It's natural to wonder if taking time out for your own spiritual wellbeing is self-indulgent when there is so much need in the world, and you may have family or other responsibilities to consider. There is also, even in Christian circles, an idea that taking time on retreat avoids the issues and problems of the 'real world', or that, by engaging in contemplative prayer (listening prayer) we are trying to 'rise above' the normal daily cares around us to some 'better', 'more spiritual' plane.

Nothing could be further from the truth. By choosing to spend quality time with God, we are actually getting *closer* to God in prayer and in love. As we listen, we allow ourselves to be changed deeply, and we glimpse something of the extent of God's love for those on the margins of society for whom each day is a struggle. As Catherine of Siena puts it:

> The secret of Christian contemplation is that it faces us with Jesus Christ *toward* our suffering world in loving service and just action.[1]

It is wise to be aware of the risk of a 'privatized' spirituality, in which the focus is on personal growth and fulfilment. Our God wants us to grow as people of course, but Godly growth invites us not only inwards to greater resourcing in God's love, but also outwards – to something bigger than ourselves, to a greater degree of connection and commitment to the world in which we live.

If you are already involved in caring for others, then there is another vital reason for making a retreat. Those in any sort of ministry or costly service who do not practise good self-care, risk 'compassion fatigue' or 'burnout'. Regular times of being alone with God, especially on a retreat, help us to be still enough for God to fill us up with whatever we need, so we can continue to be God's hands and voice to those whom we serve.

How will I find a suitable place for my retreat?

As with any holiday, deciding where to go is part of the fun, and we are often helped by other people's experiences. Because you are going on holiday with God, it makes sense to invite God into the process, asking for guidance as you look for somewhere just right. From there you might tap into your own networks of family, friends or colleagues. Someone may have a holiday home you can use, or know of a farm cottage that's vacant, or a small retreat centre which they could recommend. Don't be surprised if something 'just turns up'!

If this is really new territory for you and you don't know who to ask, then an excellent starting place if you live in the UK is

---

1 Shalem Institute: www.shalem.org/index.php/resources/quotations.

the National Retreat Association's annual publication which gives locations of retreat houses throughout the country and other helpful material. Visit their website, www.retreats.org.uk, or email them on info@retreats.org.uk. If you live out of the UK, then a look on the internet under 'Christian retreat houses', followed by your country's name, should yield a list to get you started. For readers in the United States and Canada, Spiritual Directors' International's website, www.sdiworld.org, has information about the location and suitability of retreat houses.

Once you've got some options and ideas, see how they measure up against your personal preferences and resources – consider things like:

- access to a daily rhythm of worship
- availability of Holy Communion
- whether there will be other people around or you will have a venue to yourself
- cost
- distance from home (2–3 hours' travel away is ideal)
- whether the environment respects and supports silence and solitude
- facilities – including meal arrangements or self-catering
- accessibility and safety – especially if you are ageing or disabled.

I include the latter deliberately. It's helpful to think through, for example, whether you are comfortable staying alone in an isolated area with no mobile phone coverage, or would prefer to have a room in a small retreat house where you can be independent but have the security of other people in the background.

There is no need to put yourself into a context which is stressful. After all, you are going on *holiday* with God, and that doesn't mean that you have to sleep in spartan surroundings or otherwise make yourself miserable – the sign of your devotion and longing for God is the fact that you are taking the time to listen to and be with God – there is no need for hair-shirts or their modern equivalent! You do not have to work your way into God's good books – God loves you now, completely, this very moment. Going on retreat is your love-gift to God, and an opportunity to receive, more deeply, God's love for you.

What will I do all day?

This will depend on your personal situation: any combination of sleeping, walking, intentional praying, singing, doodling, listening, more sleeping, praying with Scripture, weeping, dancing, keeping a spiritual journal, noticing, gentle creativity, more listening, still more sleeping, preparing meals, resting, reflecting, and so on. Sleep helps the body's stress hormones, chronically activated to enable us to manage over-full schedules, to switch off and go on holiday too!

In monastic rules of life such as the Rule of St Benedict, there is a balance between communal and private prayer, spiritual reading and meditation on Scripture, sleep and work. Prayers take place at regular three-hourly intervals starting at midnight with the Office of Matins and finishing with Compline at 9pm.

This pattern is *not* what most of us are called to, but it *is* an example of the way a framework can help us make the most of the time. Even if you are perfectly at ease with a day that unfolds without any structure, a good option to help you stay 'connected' to God is to let the retreat take shape around periods of intentional prayer, interspersed throughout the day at times that seem to fit your natural rhythms.

In a personal retreat context, this could look something like:

✠ a morning prayer time when you are reasonably awake
✠ a middle-of-the-day time to help centre the day in God
✠ a late-afternoon time of re-focusing and
✠ an evening opportunity to gather the gifts of the day.

Such a gentle daily rhythm is flexible, but it also signals that you are serious about your desire to hear what God is trying to 'say' to you as you go about your day and tune in to the myriad ways that God might communicate with you. To help you as you try this out, some resources for this rhythm are provided in the chapter headed Opening and Daily Prayers.

What if I get stuck in my prayer or am unsure of what to do next?

The first thing to do is to talk to God about it as honestly as you can and then to listen for guidance! Sometimes we expect a lot of ourselves and feel as if we 'ought' to be 'doing more' or 'praying harder'. In reality God just wants our company. Our whole day can be prayer if we are simply turned towards God like a sunflower following the sun. We turn up and pay loving attention to God as best we can (and I will give you some ideas of how to do that in Chapter 2, 'Making the most of your time with God'). The rest is very much up to the Spirit.

However, if you are making a personal retreat for the first time and think you really would like someone to talk to during the time you are away, then consider choosing a venue where spiritual direction is available. A trained spiritual director will help you reflect on what you sense is happening – or not happening – during your retreat. This service might incur an additional cost, but is worth it if you'd like to be able to check out what is going on with you and God as the retreat unfolds.

If you just want to be on your own for the duration of the retreat, then keeping a 'spiritual journal' will help you notice, name and deepen the experience for later reflection or discussion with your spiritual director or prayer partner.

What about taking Holy Communion?

If you come from a sacramental tradition or are used to taking Communion regularly, it is natural to want to continue this sacred practice when you are on holiday with God. How you do this will depend on your personal situation.

For some Christians there are particular protocols covering the consecration of the elements of bread and wine for Communion. If it is important to you that you abide by these protocols, you may want to talk to your priest or minister about how your desire to participate in Holy Communion while on retreat may be met. Options might include being able to attend a Communion service at the retreat house where you are staying or at a church nearby, or you may be able to take with you the Reserved Sacrament (already consecrated elements), linking you with your worshipping community back home. Another possibility would be to reconnect – in your imagination – with a significant moment of sharing Eucharist – perhaps with special people, or at a memorable place or pivotal time in your spiritual formation.

For other Christians less formalized arrangements are made for the consecration of the elements. If you are comfortable with this situation, you may want to pray imaginatively with the passage from Matthew 26.26–28 which includes the words of the institution of the Lord's Supper. Or you may simply, and in silence, follow a little liturgy which includes humble approach, penitence, reading the word of God with your heart as well as your eyes and mind, and then eating the bread and drinking the wine, aware of the 'great cloud of witnesses' who have participated in this same holy meal through the ages. Reciting the Lord's Prayer and giving thanks will bring the liturgy to a close.

Whatever you do with reverence and prayerful intention, you are not alone, for in the mystery of the Eucharist you are made one with Jesus.

What do I need to take with me?

In 2010 when I went to do a course in Jerusalem, flying from New Zealand via Hong Kong and London to Tel Aviv, I took the following in my hand luggage, each item addressing a need or allaying a fear: *A History of Jerusalem* (information); hand sanitizer, medication (health); money, travel insurance (security); passport (identity); mobile phone (connection with family); iPod (music to soothe); camera and trip book/journal (keeping my story). All of these are legitimate items of course, but it was God who really met my needs and allayed my fears as I travelled across the world on my own for the first time!

When we go on holiday with God, we are freed to travel lightly, trusting that in God we find our true security, comfort, identity, health and peace of mind; God alone will enable our memories, and help us call to mind what is important to us when we have returned home. So don't worry too much about what to take or not to take on retreat. I've known people who have taken their coffee-maker or even their sewing machine! But in reality you can travel lightly – a few clothes suitable for the time of year and the retreat setting, your Bible and a prayer book if you use one, your journal and pen/coloured pencils, music if that's an important part of your spirituality, toiletries, medication, camera, anything you need for handwork or craft and, of course, food. Self-catering has benefits, not least that you can choose what you want to eat and when.

What about taking my mobile phone and computer?

Going on holiday with God means going 'off-grid' – releasing yourself from the internet's subtle tyranny of emails, Facebook or Twitter. For some this won't pose a problem but for others the thought of being without these everyday links to social networks is highly unsettling – it is as if without them we feel incomplete. Of course, if that is the case, then it's even more reason to leave them behind. ☺

If you do choose to take a mobile phone with you, I would encourage you to keep it switched off as much as possible. Apart from a quick call home to let folk know you've arrived safely, negotiate a 'communication fast' for the duration of your retreat until you are ready to return. Otherwise, every time you receive a text message or ring home, the connection with God is inter-rupted, everyday worries resurface and the benefits of the retreat can dissipate.

If you are used to keeping your spiritual journal on your laptop then you have a choice – EITHER take the laptop with you and use it for that purpose alone, staying offline and resisting the urge to do something for work or scroll through your entire photo hoard (!) OR keep a special retreat journal using more traditional methods such as a loose-leaf folio or an exercise book which allows greater flexibility of expression. After all, leaves or flowers cannot be pressed between the pages of an iPad, nor can tears make a memory mark on a computer screen.

I am not used to being away from those I love. What if I get home-sick?

God knows and loves you and your family. If you find that you are feeling a bit sad or unsettled without loved ones near, acknowledge your homesickness and talk to God about how you feel. You may like to describe the love you have for each particular person (or pet), or the features of your home which make it familiar and a blessing to you. It doesn't matter if you cry – tears are part of prayer, especially on retreat.

There's nothing wrong with taking a photo of those you love with you. And as part of your prayer at the start of your retreat, you may want to light a candle specifically for those you've left behind, and name each one before God.

What will God do on this retreat?

Only God knows the detail, but you can be sure that God will do what is best for you, offering you a chance to experience God's tenderness and grace and helping you look at whatever gets in the way of living freely and abundantly (John 10.10). Any part of your life could come under God's loving gaze, always for your wellbeing and the building of the kingdom in and through you. For example, God may invite you, with the guidance and support of the Spirit, to go beyond your comfort zones, face an old fear, seek to forgive or be forgiven, grieve a loss or bring painful memories to the God who loves you. Some of this may sound like hard work – and it can be – but it is the way of healing, growth and greater freedom in Christ. Always remember that the great God of the universe is also infinitely kind. If you encounter something on retreat that you don't feel ready to face, just talk to God about your reluctance or anxiety. God will not force you to face anything before you are ready. Sometimes the first step towards healing is simply to acknowledge the issue and to be assured that God is *with* you in it. Then, when you are ready, an opportunity will come for you to move towards greater joy, love and peace. But a retreat is definitely not all about struggle or sadness or pain.

Preparing for your holiday with God

You may find yourself considering a new avenue of service or ministry, tapping into your God-given creativity, giving thanks for your abilities and strengths, acknowledging your need of rest, accepting – however reluctantly – that you are beautiful in the eyes of God.

For many people, life can be about trying to please others, trying to fit our round and homely selves into rigid, square expectations. In order to do this, we may have nurtured the more conventional, responsible parts of our nature, and unintentionally starved our imagination, spontaneity and creativity. In doing so, we may have lost sight of the joy God offers us, a deep joy that sustains us even when life is chaotic. So don't be surprised if going on holiday with God also means reconnecting with laughter, child-like playfulness and a renewed fascination and zest for life.

2

Making the most of your time with God

When we want to open ourselves up to God's loving and personal communication, there are a few recognized 'tips' which aid this receptivity. Several of them are described below and will provide 'ways in' if you want some ideas about how to deepen your communication with God.

Seeking prayer support

In this very individualistic society, we often struggle to ask other people for what we need, even when it comes to prayer. However, when we go on holiday with God, it is important for our own spiritual wellbeing that we set independence aside and ask others to pray for us. The supportive prayer of two or three trusted mature Christians weaves a protective cloak for us, reminding us of God's grace and helping us know deeply within our spirit that we are held close to the heart of God.

It is also an exercise in humility to name the fears or concerns we have and to bring these to others for prayer. To acknowledge, for example, that we are nervous about driving 200 miles to a retreat house or that we are uncertain about how family or workmates might manage while we are away, allows us to face these realities and bring them honestly before God. In this way, such concerns are identified *before* we leave home, and are less likely to act as distractions while we are away, because we know that prayer 'covers' those we love.

If, however, you don't have anyone around you who can uphold you, talk to God about your desire for prayer support. God will provide even if you have no idea how or who.

Introducing contemplation

The term 'contemplation' is used in two ways in this book:

ℵ the act of noticing, looking intently, lovingly, at something that has gained our attention, just as a young child might spend time closely examining a flower or looking in a rock pool; and

ℵ that state of receptive, wordless prayer in which we open ourselves to the direct work of the Spirit in us.

So let's explore each one in turn.

When we are on holiday with God we are moving at a gentler pace, so when something does catch our attention, we have the time to pause and enter more fully into a particular moment, giving space for God to use it to 'speak' to us.

I remember a recent experience on a two-day retreat. The second morning, as I was walking outside after a heavy downpour of rain, my attention was drawn to a sparrow in a puddle. As I paused and watched, this sparrow dipped and shook, splashed and hopped, having a great bath. I found myself wondering at the way the sparrow and the puddle came together in that moment. After all, the sparrow hadn't woken that morning and decided that at 11.10am he would go to a particular puddle and make his ablutions! Instead he had simply enjoyed what was provided in that moment. Through the antics of this squeaky-clean sparrow, came the reassuring 'message' for me: God loves me and will provide for me during the day. I don't have to work hard to order every detail or micro-manage how I can find what nourishes me – God will nourish me, if I am open enough to notice and enjoy the gifts of grace around me.

I had been struggling to find a way to resource myself regularly in the middle of demanding pastoral ministry, so this came as a welcome and timely reminder that resourcing is what *God* does. You and I can trust God, who knows us better than we know ourselves, to give us what we need at intervals during the day. Our part is to *recognize and receive* God's provision and guidance, and we can do this only if we take moments of stillness, slow down periodically, and keep our interior listening space clear of anxious clutter!

When we begin to explore those *simple moments which attract our attention*, we are opening ourselves up to God's communication with us **in the midst of everyday life**. God can use **anything**: the creation, other people, our circumstances, patterns of events or synchronicity, the media and art forms, our own inner sense of peace, as well as Scripture, reason and tradition to guide and encourage, challenge or correct us. The simplest thing – a worker demolishing a wall, a gardener turning over the earth, a child examining a plum before spreading vibrant purple over face, hands, highchair – can be a vehicle of grace if we stop, ponder and allow the Spirit to touch and teach our spirit.

The second way that 'contemplation' is used in this book refers to that state of heart-felt, wordless, silent availability to God, as the Holy Spirit works *deeply* and *directly* with our spirit. There is no activity of the intellect, no making of connections by our efforts of thought or imagination. It's a form of prayer perhaps expressed most simply in the words of an old man who came daily to a church to pray at the altar of the Blessed Sacrament. When his priest, the Curé d'Ars,[2] asked him what he was doing, he replied:

'I look at Him, and He looks at me.'

Striking in its simplicity, this brief description encapsulates the way a person's humble adoration of Jesus is grace-fully received as the gentle power of God's Spirit melts inner resistance and strengthens the believer in holiness. This form of contemplation is not reserved for a spiritual élite, but for you and me, ordinary people who long for a deep connection with Christ.

As we shall see in the next section, contemplation can also form a natural part of praying with Scripture using *lectio divina*, as well as being a standalone prayer practice. This form of contemplative prayer is sometimes called centring prayer[3] or Christian meditation,[4] in which we set aside spoken prayer and use an

2 St John Vianney, the patron saint of parish priests.
3 See the work and teaching of Thomas Keating and Cynthia Bourgeault.
4 See the work and teaching of John Main and Lawrence Freeman.

anchor phrase such as *maranatha* (Come, Lord Jesus), a word of Scripture such as *abide* or the name of *Jesus* to help our wandering mind gently return to being open to God in our innermost being.

Praying with Scripture

You may be used to studying Scripture, perhaps in a group setting, or on your own with the help of a reading plan and a commentary on the day's readings. Retreat time is a good opportunity to build on that experience by using Scripture as a catalyst for your prayer. But even if you have never spent a lot of time with Scripture, trying out *lectio divina* (sacred reading) or *praying with the imagination* can be a revelation.

Lectio divina – an ancient spiritual practice now finding new acceptance across Christian denominations. It consists of four elements which weave together like a braided river to help us move deeper in our understanding of Scripture and our relationship with God. The prayerful process includes:

Lectio – a very slow reading of a small portion of Scripture several times, preferably aloud, giving space for the Spirit to 'quicken' a verse.

Meditatio – pondering a word or phrase that has 'lit up' as we have been reading, making connections with our situation, allowing the Spirit to guide our associations and reflections.

Oratio – responding to God from the heart, using vocal prayer, movement, singing, writing or some other form of honest expression that suits the moment and your personality.

Contemplatio – resting from thinking or active prayer, allowing our mind to quieten so that we can simply be with God, letting our spirit be open to the gentle touch of the Spirit.

Lectio divina nourishes us so that we can be there for others. Whether or not we *feel* anything during this prayer practice is immaterial; we are making ourselves fully available to the work of God in our inner being. *Lectio* can lead to a fifth element, *actio*, in which we ask God to enable the gifts we've received in this prayer time to be expressed in our everyday world, so we may become makers of peace and bringers of justice to others.

Praying with the imagination – using our mind's ability to form inner pictures or impressions so that a familiar Scripture passage can be given space to take on new life as we place ourselves in the story and interact with the characters as if we were present. Most of us have a hurdle to overcome before praying this way, because we have been told off as children for 'imagining things' or warned as adults that flights of the imagination can lure us away from God. In this context, however, we are asking the Spirit to guide our prayer time as we use our God-given imagination to help us draw closer to God.

Praying with Gospel passages where Jesus is present can be particularly rich and revealing. The process is straightforward:

Pray – ask for the Spirit's guidance and protection.

Choose – a suitable passage (see the themed resources in Chapter 5 for examples).

Read – the passage two or three times so it becomes familiar.

Use your senses – let the scene unfold in your mind or get an inner impression of the context, who is present, where it is and so on.

Enter the story – imagine you are present, as an observer or participant, allowing the story to unfold until it comes to a natural ending.

Reflect – on what you have experienced or, if not a lot 'happened', notice how you are feeling and bring that to God in prayer.

Old Testament passages or portions of the Psalms can also be extremely helpful, as a personal example might illustrate:

Years ago, I was praying with Isaiah 43.1–4 at the start of a Week of Guided Prayer. The word 'redeemed' had taken my attention and as I sat quietly, a picture of the dim interior of a pawn-broker's shop formed in my mind. I sensed that I – as a very small child – was on a high shelf, behind the counter. Jesus, dressed in a white shirt and jeans, came into the shop and spoke to the man behind the counter. I heard Jesus say, 'She looks all right to me.' As they shook hands to seal the purchase, I could see the marks of nails in Jesus' hands – I knew inwardly that the price he had paid was to take upon himself all my anger and grief, my struggles and my failings. Jesus lifted me off the shelf and took me outside, where we sat together on a bench in the sunshine.

This moment was pivotal on my spiritual journey because it enabled that most necessary connection – the one between head and heart. Through this imaginative encounter, which I didn't anticipate or make up in any way, Jesus became *real* for me, **really real**, and I *knew* at a deeper level the truth of the work of Christ on the cross, and the meaning of redemption.

We never know what will happen when we use our imagination in this way, but praying with Scripture, using our senses and our mind's creativity, can often open up new levels of awareness and deeper appreciation of what is really going on between Jesus and the participants in the passage. And by extension, it can help us notice what is significant for us, in our own situations.

Keeping a spiritual journal

If you've ever been on an overseas holiday, you'll know the benefits of keeping a 'trip book' to help you remember the events of each day. Keeping a spiritual journal while on retreat serves a similar purpose, because although we think we will remember the ways God meets us, it is surprisingly easy for us to forget once we are back in the thick of 'normal' life again. A spiritual journal helps us recall God's activity in our lives, *and* helps us discover more about ourselves in the process. As such, it is an important aid to spiritual growth and a source of comfort and reassurance when we meet times of dryness or doubt.

The content of a spiritual journal focuses on our interaction and growing relationship with God; it can include whatever we want to put into it as we unpack strong feelings, explore dreams, savour snippets of Scripture, press leaves or flowers from a special place, record lyrics to a song that has touched our heart, write a prayer-poem, wonder and question, pray, draw or doodle ... If you don't find it easy to put pen to paper, the good news is that when you keep a spiritual journal, there are no rules governing how it 'ought' to be done. So don't worry about spelling or punctuation or presentation. You can even use 'text' language if you like! The themed resources in Chapter 5 each contain a range of reflection starters for you to explore – an ideal way to begin keeping a spiritual journal!

Reviewing the day

One of the great pleasures of being on holiday is sitting down at the end of the day and thinking back over the discoveries, challenges and joys that day has brought. Whether we do this with a coffee after dinner or tucked up in bed before sleep, the same process is valuable when on holiday with God.

Instead of places seen and new foods tasted, we prayerfully review where we have been most aware of God during the day, and we note anything that has taken us further away from God. We consider too where we have felt energy and hopefulness and where we have felt drained or discouraged. By practising this simple *examen* (review) we are building up self-awareness and the ability to notice patterns in our responses, prayer or inner struggles which we can bring to God in our night prayer.

3

Setting off and settling in

The retreat begins as soon as you leave home

It's unrealistic to expect to go smoothly and rapidly from urban busyness or rural routines to a state of prayerful attentiveness to God. Even if you have a stable set of prayer practices which bring you to stillness on a daily basis, you will still need time to adjust your pace, to make the transition from a packed schedule to a less structured day. The journey to the retreat destination becomes a key part of that shift of focus.

The morning I was due to leave for a retreat last year, I woke struggling with the question of destination. Was it to be the planned time at our cottage near Lake Taupo, a drive of three and a half hours, or, because I was really tired, should I make a change and see if I could go to a friend's house near Onaero beach only half an hour away from home? I went to my morning prayer-time with my mind rehearsing logical reasons in favour of the nearer destination. As I became still, the words of the carol 'Little donkey' came to mind. This children's song speaks of Mary's journey to Bethlehem, all the more vivid for me since my visit to the Holy Land earlier that year. Mary was the Christ-bearer and her journey wasn't short and convenient. It was long and uncomfortable, but gave her plenty of time to reflect. As I let the words reach into my own situation, I realized it was important that I took the longer option, because God was inviting me – as God invites us all – to be Christ-bearers in the world. Allowing whatever God is forming within us to come to birth often takes effort, takes time. And so I chose the longer road.

Almost as soon as I had driven beyond Onaero, God started journeying with me, challenging me to share my time and not be afraid to pick up two young hitchhikers, and then slowing me down with roadworks, and more roadworks, and a succession of slow vehicles so I could not speed towards my destination. Instead I drove by fields of buttercups, and broom, until I was driving the last few miles with yellow flowers like ribbons welcoming me to this holiday with God. The drive took four and a half hours, but it didn't matter because I knew the Spirit was with me, helping me face a fear, slowing my busy pace, preparing me for more of God.

A trip of three or four hours can be an ideal oasis between ordinary routines and the retreat, if you trust that God will use the time to bless, gently challenge, and enrich you.

Arriving and slowing down

After you have checked out your accommodation, unloaded, unpacked and made a cuppa (!), it will be time to explore your immediate environment. One of the first things is to find a space which can become your sacred place for prayer and reflection. Naturally you can pray anywhere, but many people find it helpful to have somewhere 'set aside', somewhere to light a candle as a symbol of Christ's presence, to place an icon or cross, or add things you come across during the retreat which have meaning for you. If the weather and location permit, this might be a place outdoors which becomes for you a simple sanctuary; if it's cold and barren outside, somewhere cosy indoors might appeal.

Once the practicalities are out of the way and you feel ready, it is time to open your heart to God, to share as honestly as you can how you are feeling and what has brought you to this moment.

Resources to help you begin the retreat are in Chapter 4, 'Opening and daily prayers'.

Because most of us spend our lives rushing from one thing to another, it can feel totally foreign to have an 'empty space' lying before us like an unexpected blank page in a book full of action. Our time is often regulated, spoken for, costly, and insufficient for the tasks that present themselves to us each day. But time on holiday with God is not bound by hours and minutes. It can be described as *kairos* time – the 'right' time when God meets us, a spacious time which unfolds gently, slowly.

Setting off and settling in

To help you navigate this paradigm shift in the pace of life as you begin your retreat, here are some ideas:

ॐ Take off your watch. It seems strange at first but it gives a great sense of freedom, and encourages you just to do and be what comes naturally.

ॐ Embrace 'slow cooking'. Take your time in meal preparation, allowing yourself space to engage with whatever you are doing, whether it be chopping carrots for a stew or making a sandwich.

ॐ Resolve to read *aloud* any scriptures or prayers. Most of us habitually speed read; reading aloud helps to slow you down so you can really see and hear the text.

ॐ If you have brought music with you, listen to some relaxing music, or sing a chant (for example, Taizé, Margaret Rizza).

ॐ If you are struggling with slowing down, stop now and then and take a few deep breaths.

ॐ Deliberately slow down the pace of your walking.

All of these are practical helps to slow you down, but what *really* makes a difference is a change in focus, from yourself to God. Habituated as we all are to thinking about things from our own perspective, we can learn from the example of Brother Lawrence,[5] a seventeenth-century French lay brother. Whether working in the kitchen or walking or gardening, he cultivated a conscious awareness of the presence of God by making an 'interior glance' towards God whenever he could. God was lovingly brought to mind over and over again, and in this way was woven into the fabric of every hour, every minute, until Br Lawrence lived in constant connection with God.

If, like Br Lawrence, you do everything 'for the love of God', the pace at which you live your life will change. You will be reconnected with the truth of God's abiding presence, and develop a capacity to 'be' where you are, for it is in the *present moment* that you meet your God.

---

5 Br Lawrence's spiritual guidance remains accessible through his letters, published as *The Practice of the Presence of God*, available in many editions and reprints.

Being guided by the Spirit

As you slow down, as the inner chatter quietens, you will be better able to hear the 'voice' of the Spirit of God, the Comforter who will remind you of what Jesus wants you to know (John 14.26). This touch of the Spirit may come to you in a variety of ways:

- ꙮ as a thought giving encouragement or guidance
- ꙮ as an interior 'nudge' or 'prompt' to action
- ꙮ by enlivening Scripture as you pray with the Word
- ꙮ by the timing of external events
- ꙮ in an inner 'conversation' directly with Jesus
- ꙮ by an unfolding awareness of a deeper, spiritual meaning to what you are reading, listening to or seeing
- ꙮ in a graced moment of felt encounter with God
- ꙮ by an inner knowing of the next step – not through planning or analysis but by a simple response to what is happening in the moment
- ꙮ through the welling up of tears and/or praise
- ꙮ by a growing sense of inner peace or release from strain.

There may well be other ways by which God's Spirit will touch you while on retreat, but this list may help you notice the gentle but purposeful hand of God reaching into your reality.

Resistance

It seems a strange thing to say, but even when we have made a clear decision to spend time with God on retreat, we can still make choices that keep God at arm's length. We can be caught in contrariness: even though our hearts and minds long for God-connection, our wills often run in the opposite direction, subtly but resolutely resisting facing the God who waits, faithfully, patiently. We can understand why Paul wrote in Romans 7:

> [15]I do not understand my own actions. For I do not do what I want, but I do the very thing I hate ...

²¹So I find it to be a law that when I want to do what is good, evil lies close at hand. ²²For I delight in the law of God in my inmost self, ²³but I see in my members another law at war with the law of my mind, making me captive to the law of sin that dwells in my members.

If Paul's words strike a chord with you, if you recognize that there are times when you could spend quality time with God but instead you choose something else, then one of the first things to do when you begin your retreat is to talk to God about this inner struggle and about your desire for more of God in your life.

God is I AM, fully present to you in what de Caussade calls 'the sacrament of the present moment'. When God calls his chosen ones in Scripture, their response is often, 'Here I am ...' [6] Such a simple statement, but that's what God wants to hear from you too: 'Here I am'. Not dreaming of a fantastic future, dwelling on the highs and lows of the past, nor caught up in current problems, but simply present, attentive to God. If you make yourself fully available to God, your mind is receptive to the whispers of the Spirit; your eyes are open to the God who speaks volumes through what you notice around you; your heart is sensitive to the wonder of creation or the words of Scripture.

Tears and dancing

Retreat time is often surprisingly emotional – and I don't mean that in a negative sense. Perhaps it's because there is no one else around or because we have slowed down long enough to listen to our thoughts and are quiet enough to hear the whispers of the Spirit, but it has been my experience as a retreat director, and as a retreatant, that God often helps us release our feelings during this set-apart time. Heights and depths of emotion can be faced and safely expressed under the guidance of the Spirit. So if you find tears welling up while on retreat, remember that God desires your wellbeing and is with you as you weep, whether your tears arise from inner anguish, dreadful loss, fear or frustration:

---

6 For example, Moses (Exodus 3), Samuel (1 Samuel 3) Mary (Luke 1).

You have kept count of my tossings;
put my tears in your bottle.
Are they not in your record?
(Psalm 56.8)

What a picture of deepest care and concern – your God watches over you when you feel alone in the darkest moments of the night. Your God knows how many tears you weep, down to the last salty trickle down your cheeks.

Sometimes, however, your tears will spring not from pain or loss but from surprising joy, from being moved by the love of God tenderly touching your soul. Such tears of joy or wonder may even trigger the desire to dance. If you feel a bit foolish or shy about dancing alone, hugging a big cushion helps! The physical freedom of dancing helps you express the love you feel towards God. In giving yourself to the movement (with or without music), your body can delight in God and you can sense God delighting in you as you experience the reality of Psalm 30.11–12:

You have turned my mourning into dancing;
you have taken off my sackcloth
and clothed me with joy,
so that my soul may praise you and not be silent.
O LORD my God, I will give thanks to you forever.

Dreaming

The biblical record contains many examples of dreams being used to guide, warn, encourage and support people of faith, so God might use dreams to do the same for us while we are on retreat.

Dreams help us tap into a deeper knowing than we can access in our conscious life. If you have what you consider to be a 'dream of interest', then you can begin to work with it by writing the dream in the first person present tense, for example, 'I am walking along a road which has high hedges on each side ...' Then follow the simple sequence proposed by Savary, Berne and Williams (1984):[7]

---

7 Louis M. Savary, Patricia H. Berne and Strephon Kaplan Williams, *Dreams and Spiritual Growth: A Judeo-Christian Approach to Dreamwork*, New York: Paulist Press, 1984, pp. 22–5.

T   Give your dream a title.

T   Identify any clear theme/themes.

A   Note down your feelings (affect) in the dream.

Q   Note any questions that the dream raises for you.

From there it may help to identify any symbols in the dream and what these might mean *to you*. Only you know what special significance a particular symbol might have, so only you can interpret your dream.

A few notes about dreams:

ॐ   Dream content is usually symbolic not literal – the exception being dreams that originate from trauma. Such post-traumatic dreaming is experienced as troubling replays of the traumatic event and usually needs therapeutic intervention.

ॐ   Dream characters are usually aspects of the dreamer's personality being given a visible reality, rather than saying something about other people.

ॐ   Rarely are dreams predictive – they normally help us process material from our daily life or show us areas where we need to do some emotional work. If dreams or nightmares reoccur it is because we haven't paid attention to the core elements and what they might want to teach us about our emotions, inner wellbeing and relational capacity.

God can use dreams to bypass the rational mind, if the dreamer is not making progress with a decision or is finding it hard to sort out priorities or make choices. I think of a time when I went on retreat feeling particularly exhausted and unsettled about a planned holiday with my husband to Avila in Spain. Three nights into the retreat I had a dream of such clarity that I immediately woke up (at 4am) and wrote the dream down – here is the extract from my journal:

My husband and I are house-hunting though not really expecting to move. We are offered 'two for one' – two homes on the same plot of land up on an elevated site (a bonus!). The first one was old, like a villa (!!), but once inside it had several levels and was light and spacious. We go upstairs and open the door of one of the rooms as I say to John, 'This could be a retreat place.'

The room is big enough to *dance* in, a large oval-shape room, and I sense wonder, excitement, potential ...

The predominant feeling is of emerging joy ...

A second dream snippet that same night followed:

I am walking down a road near a worker's van. Inside was a scary black dog but he didn't jump out at me when the door was opened.

'We are going to Avila' was my simple conclusion – the strong sense of hopefulness and possibility and joy associated with the opportunity to explore 'a villa'/Avila in the first dream, together with the 'empty fear' theme portrayed in the second dream snippet, helped me settle on the course of action I had been struggling with before I came on retreat.

Maybe a dream will form an important and helpful part of your retreat time!

4

Opening and daily prayers

This chapter begins with prayers from which to choose as you settle into a gentle rhythm for each day. There are examples to cover the opening of the retreat, as well as 'getting up' prayers, prayers at midday and late afternoon, and 'going to bed' prayers.

A prayer pattern for the closing of the retreat is on page 139.

You may, of course, prefer to use your own prayers or have some favourites you've brought with you which seem fitting.

A prayer upon arrival

O God of the ages,
Lover of my soul.

Take my intention
to listen and learn from your Spirit,
and hallow it,
so I may grow in your grace,
like a seed in rich soil.

Release my imagination,
inspire my creativity,
soothe my restlessness,
salve my sorrow,
so I may settle,
quietly, peacefully,
into the warmth of your love,
and know myself
blessed.
AMEN

Opening and daily prayers

Starting the Retreat – Here I am O God

From the following pages, choose either the Exodus 3.1–14 passage (Moses – the burning bush) or the 1 Samuel 3.1–10 passage (God calls Samuel).

In your prayer place, light a 'Christ' candle.

Here I am O God.
I am not sure what will happen,
what we will see and do together,
but I choose to trust your love for me
made visible in Jesus, my friend and brother.

Before you read the chosen passage slowly, aloud, pray:

As these words are spoken,
may they strengthen my being, and nurture my spirit
through the grace of your love. AMEN

Read the passage aloud and then spend five minutes in silent reflection …

Here I am O God.
Like the young Samuel and the old Moses
I am stepping aside and taking time to listen
to your word for me, to your joy in me,
to your blessing of me, and your gentle challenge.

This is what I bring with me …

Name before God any concerns, any personal issues which you know need to be addressed, and any deep longings that are bubbling inside you.

This is how I feel and what I think I need …

Name before God your honest feelings, and what you sense you need for the day – practical things, insight, hope … whatever comes as you pray.

May all that gives me concern be held in your hands.
May I be open to your work in my life during this retreat.
Help me to welcome what you offer of yourself
as I listen and learn, guided and protected by your Spirit. AMEN

33

Exodus 3.1–14 – Moses and the burning bush

¹Moses was keeping the flock of his father-in-law Jethro, the priest of Midian; he led his flock beyond the wilderness, and came to Horeb, the mountain of God. ²There the angel of the LORD appeared to him in a flame of fire out of a bush; he looked, and the bush was blazing, yet it was not consumed. ³Then Moses said, 'I must turn aside and look at this great sight, and see why this bush is not burned up.' ⁴When the LORD saw that he had turned aside to see, God called to him out of the bush, 'Moses. Moses!'

And he said, 'Here I am.' ⁵Then he said, 'Come no closer! Remove the sandals from your feet, for the place on which you are standing is holy ground.' ⁶He said further, 'I am the God of your father, the God of Abraham, the God of Isaac, and the God of Jacob.' And Moses hid his face, for he was afraid to look at God.

⁷Then the LORD said, 'I have observed the misery of my people who are in Egypt; I have heard their cry on account of their taskmasters. Indeed, I know their sufferings, ⁸and I have come down to deliver them from the Egyptians, and to bring them up out of that land to a good and broad land, a land flowing with milk and honey ...

⁹The cry of the Israelites has now come to me; I have also seen how the Egyptians oppress them. ¹⁰So come, I will send you to Pharaoh to bring my people, the Israelites, out of Egypt.' ¹¹But Moses said to God, 'Who am I that I should go to Pharaoh, and bring the Israelites out of Egypt?' ¹²He said, 'I will be with you; and this shall be the sign for you that it is I who sent you: when you have brought the people out of Egypt, you shall worship God on this mountain.' ¹³But Moses said to God, 'If I come to the Israelites and say to them, "The God of your ancestors has sent me to you," and they ask me, "What is his name?" what shall I say to them?' ¹⁴God said to Moses, 'I AM WHO I AM.' He said further, 'Thus you shall say to the Israelites, "I AM has sent me to you."'

1 Samuel 3.1–10 – The call of Samuel

¹Now the boy Samuel was ministering to the LORD under Eli. The word of the LORD was rare in those days; visions were not widespread.

²At that time Eli, whose eyesight had begun to grow dim so that he could not see, was lying down in his room; ³the lamp of God had not yet gone out, and Samuel was lying down in the temple of the LORD, where the ark of God was. ⁴Then the LORD called, 'Samuel! Samuel!' and he said, 'Here I am!' ⁵and ran to Eli, and said, 'Here I am, for you called me.' But he said, 'I did not call; lie down again.' So he went and lay down. ⁶The LORD called again, 'Samuel!' Samuel got up and went to Eli, and said, 'Here I am, for you called me.' But he said, 'I did not call, my son; lie down again.' ⁷Now Samuel did not yet know the LORD, and the word of the LORD had not yet been revealed to him. ⁸The LORD called Samuel again, a third time. And he got up and went to Eli, and said, 'Here I am, for you called me.' Then Eli perceived that the LORD was calling the boy. ⁹Therefore Eli said to Samuel, 'Go, lie down; and if he calls you, you shall say, "Speak, LORD, for your servant is listening."' So Samuel went and lay down in his place.

¹⁰Now the LORD came and stood there, calling as before, 'Samuel! Samuel!' And Samuel said, 'Speak, for your servant is listening.'

Gentle rhythm for the day – Getting Up Prayers

You may have your own set of prayers but, if not, choose one of the following and add the Lord's Prayer if you wish, or the Prayer of Richard of Chichester.

Good morning, God.
Thank you for breath and life this day.
Please be with those I love,
and with those who are lonely.
Wrap us all in the warmth of your faithful love,
and help me to be open to your life in me.
Through Jesus our friend and brother.
AMEN

This day, O God, I give you thanks
for eyes to see and ears to hear,
for mind and will to offer you,
for the wonder of this place and time,
for the gift of your Son Jesus.
May your Spirit dance with me this day.
AMEN

Here I am, loving God.
I am not good at mornings –
they come round so quickly and
my bed is so warm.
But here I am, O Holy One.
Wake me up to your light,
shine in all my dark places
and brighten my soul this day,
through Jesus, Light of the World.
AMEN

The Lord's Prayer

Our Father in heaven,
  hallowed be your name,
  your kingdom come,
  your will be done, on earth as in heaven.
Give us today our daily bread.
Forgive us our sins
  as we forgive those who sin against us.
Save us from the time of trial
  and deliver us from evil.
For the kingdom, the power, and the glory are yours
  now and for ever.
AMEN

The Prayer of Richard of Chichester

Thanks be to thee, my Lord Jesus Christ,
  for all the benefits thou hast given me,
  for all the pains and insults thou hast borne
  for me.
O most merciful redeemer, friend and brother,
  may I know thee more clearly,
  love thee more dearly,
  and follow thee more nearly,
  day by day.
AMEN

Gentle rhythm for the day – Middle of the Day Prayers

You may want to say this prayer somewhere out of doors if the weather is fine. If not, then bring inside a symbol of the natural world – a twig, or leaf or flower, or water from a stream or the sea, and set it in your prayer place.

Dear God
I am not at the beginning of my life
nor yet, I hope, at its ending,
but somewhere in the middle.
You know my past, and you hold
my future in kind and steady hands.
Help me to live fully in the present
even if these middle years
are full of change and challenge.
AMEN

My friend Jesus,
did you stop in the middle of
a busy day of walking and teaching
and healing and holding?
Help me to stop for a moment –
to breathe in the stillness
and name my heart's longing.
In the middle of the busyness
may I reclaim your Presence,
which brings beauty and hope
into my muddled world.
AMEN

The day lies poised between what has been
and what will be.
Balance me O God
on the pivot of your peace.
AMEN

Gentle rhythm for the day – Late Afternoon Prayers

This may be the time you choose to include Holy Communion, using a form appropriate for your denomination or using the words of Matthew 26.26–28.

Or you may want to acknowledge what the day has brought so far, some aspect of discovery, delight or struggle that has unfolded.

O God,

I come full of surprises, of gratitude, of questions ...

I have discovered something about you I did not know ...

I have discovered something about myself I did not know ...

You are all Wisdom.
You hold my knowing and unknowing in tender tension,
keeping me within the safety of your Spirit.
Soothe me, stretch me, secure me in your Love.
AMEN

A Prayer for Generosity – St Ignatius of Loyola

Lord, teach me to be generous.
Teach me to serve you as you deserve;
to give and not to count the cost,
to fight and not to heed the wounds,
to toil and not to seek for rest,
to labour and not to ask for reward,
save that of knowing that I do your will.
AMEN

Gentle rhythm for the day – Going to Bed Prayers

The spiritual practice of the examen – reflection at day's end – is a helpful way to end the day. Consider what has brought you closer to God or taken you further away. Bring to God what you have discovered and any questions or patterns which you begin to see emerging. Then use one of the following or make up your own 'going to bed' prayer.

Sometimes I am afraid of the dark.
I am an adult and this should not be so,
but sometimes it is my truth.
This night O God,
hold my small and shaky soul
in the palm of your hand.
Calm all my fears,
banish my imaginary crises
and worst-case scenarios, and
replace them with a sense of
your peace and protection,
that I may rest,
blessed.
AMEN

Here I am, O God.
Another day has passed and I am none the wiser, or so it seems.
But you, O God, are Wisdom, and so I lean on you.
Guide my wonderings until they melt into your Truth,
into that Love which tends my soul
and warms the universe.
AMEN

It is dark, O Light of the world.
I am in need of your illumination,
your warmth and love, this night.
Shine on me, in me, through me,
that I may be a small but steady light
in someone else's darkness.
AMEN

5

Themed resources for your personal retreat

In this chapter you will find ten 'traditional' holiday destinations or activities, each linked to a Gospel story and highlighting a particular aspect of the spiritual journey. Ask the Holy Spirit to help you identify one that is right for you at this moment. If it seems a surprising choice, just go with it and see what happens, remembering that God always has your greatest good in mind.

The material for each destination or situation begins with a **focus verse** from Scripture. This 'sets the scene' and may become a breath prayer and companion for you through the day. For each theme, an **opening prayer** is offered, followed by the full text of a Scripture passage to pray with using *lectio divina* or **imaginative prayer**. On retreat you have time to give to this process, room for the Spirit to work within your receptive mind and heart.

Once you have spent time praying with the passage, engage with one or two of the **personal reflection questions**. You may want to do some writing or drawing in your journal, noticing what the passage might have to say to *your* particular situation, before you read **further food for thought** in which the theme is unpacked.

Each of the themed resources then offers some suggestions for **deepening** – ways of creating space for the Spirit to help you integrate your discoveries with your own personal story and faith journey. Choose one or two of the options; no need to do them all, unless you feel that they are especially valuable for you at this time. Some options can only be done once you return home from your retreat. A **closing prayer** brings the time to an end, but again, you can use your own prayer – whatever is fitting.

It may be that the first themed material you choose will be enough for your prayer and reflection for the whole retreat. If not,

there is no need to work hard to make meaning from a passage; just allow the Spirit to guide you to another focus for the next period of intentional prayer.

The places and associated themes to choose from are

At the lake's edge	*developing trust*
Waiting	*learning to 'be still'*
In the marketplace	*setting priorities*
On the water	*dealing with fear*
Gallery or garden	*appreciating beauty*
Walking	*making a pilgrimage*
Being adventurous	*risk-taking*
Anywhere	*meeting the marginalized*
Facing the unexpected	*suffering*
Eating together	*growing in intimacy*
By the pool	*opening to healing*
On the mountain top	*choosing to listen*

On holiday with God

At the lake's edge – *developing trust*

Focus verse

Trust in the LORD with all your heart,
and do not rely on your own insight.
In all your ways acknowledge him,
and he will make straight your paths.
(Proverbs 3.5–6)

Opening prayer

O God, how I long to trust you with all of myself
and with those I love.
Water the seed of trust within me,
that it may grow, and I with it.
AMEN

Scripture to use for lectio divina *or imaginative prayer*

[1]Once while Jesus was standing beside the Lake of Gennesaret, and the crowd were pressing in on him to hear the word of God, [2]he saw two boats at the shore of the lake; the fishermen had gone out of them and were washing their nets. [3]He got into one of the boats, the one belonging to Simon, and asked him to put out a little way from the shore. Then he sat down and taught the crowds from the boat. [4]When he had finished speaking, he said to Simon, 'Put out into the deep water, and let down your nets for a catch.' [5]Simon answered, 'Master, we have worked all night but have caught nothing. Yet if you say so, I will let down the nets.' [6]When they had done this, they caught so many fish that their nets were beginning to break. [7]So they signalled their partners in the other boat to come and help them. And they came and filled both boats, so that they began to sink. [8]But when Simon Peter saw this, he fell down at Jesus' knees and said, 'Go away from me, Lord, for I am a sinful man!' [9]For he and all who were with him were

amazed at the catch of fish that they had taken; ¹⁰and so also were James and John, the sons of Zebedee, who were partners with Simon. Then Jesus said to Simon, 'Do not be afraid; from now on you will be catching people.' ¹¹When they had brought their boats to shore, they left everything and followed him. (Luke 5.1–11)

Personal reflection

🙨 What has touched my heart/sparked my imagination in this passage?

🙨 How have I been surprised, even challenged, by Jesus?

Further food for thought

Peter's day had started with disappointment – a night's fishing with his friends had yielded nothing for them to take home to their families. Perhaps it was a welcome diversion when the repetitive task of mending nets was interrupted by a simple request from Jesus – to go a 'little way' from the shore. So Peter takes him out on the lake and finds himself listening as Jesus speaks to the gathered people, his voice travelling cleanly across the water to rest in ready hearts.

Suddenly, Jesus surprises and challenges Peter to fish again. Recalling the empty boats returning to shore at dawn, Peter respectfully voices his uncertainty. For a few heartbeats Peter stands on the threshold of a fundamental decision: to consent or resist. Then, acknowledging that it is *Jesus* who is asking him to do this seemingly pointless task, Peter obeys.

What follows astounds them all. The huge catch draws Peter beyond sheer amazement to a deeper awareness of the true nature of Jesus as 'holy', as 'other'. Peter instinctively knows that he is not fit to share the same space as Jesus, or breathe the same air. Painfully aware of his wretchedness, he asks Jesus to leave him. Instead Jesus reaches out to heal his sense of shame and fear, drawing him closer, inviting him to share his life and ministry.

Jesus trusts Peter to become the person he was created to be, the rock on which Jesus would found the church – in time.

Jesus trusts you too – to be fully the person you have been created to be, with your unique story, struggles and giftings.

How does this journey of deepening trust unfold?

In Peter's case, Jesus began to build trust, not by asking him to do something unreasonable, or well beyond his abilities. Instead Jesus started where Peter was, both literally and figuratively, 'at the lake's edge'. They first go 'a little way' and then he invites Peter into 'deeper water' – a metaphor that clearly reminds us of the call of Christ to follow wherever he leads us. Once back on shore, the simple invitation to follow Jesus at that moment was given, and Peter responded. That decision would, of course, lead to all sorts of situations in which Peter would be invited to expand his understanding of God, of himself and of his role in the establishment of the church of Christ. But at this point, all Peter is able to do, he does. He gives his 'yes' to Jesus and takes the next step on his 'trust in God' journey.

Jesus invites you to an ongoing journey of learning to trust him, and that journey has already begun. You have given your 'yes' to Jesus and taken this chance to come away on retreat. Your 'trust in God' journey – and mine – develops as we learn to trust God for small things first and then gradually for things that require more of us. This process gently builds our capacity to live with more freedom and less anxiety. At first we may be like little children at the lake's edge, with our mum or dad standing thigh deep in the water, beckoning us to come and play. Some of us hesitate, fearful of the cold or the depth or the splashing or the leaving behind of solid ground or even unsure if our parent will keep us safe; some of us simply step forward with confidence – literally with faith – knowing from experience that our parent is trustworthy and it will be fun!

Our childhood experiences have a big impact on how we see God and whether we consider God to be trustworthy. For those of us who had reliable, loving caregivers and no childhood trauma, our journey of trust can move relatively smoothly from infancy to adulthood, and we carry with us a sense of confidence in our ability to function well in the world. We have experienced the powerful parent, who is like God to us when we are little, as kind and 'on our side', and so we are more able to see God's goodness and firm, faithful care.

However, for others of us, our capacity to trust has been diminished by the unpredictability of unstable caregivers, through abuse, neglect or abandonment. The tragic implication of this for our 'trust in God' journey is that we may have unconsciously transferred some of those negative behaviours and attitudes onto God. Instead of drawing ever closer to a kind and reliable God, we run away from, or at least keep our emotional distance from, a God who, we fearfully think, is a bully like our erratic early caregivers: alternately indifferent and demanding, undermining our sense of our own goodness, and never satisfied, no matter how hard we try to please.

The good news is that in the life and work of Jesus, we come to see that God is *not* a bully. At the core of God's nature is a heart of unconditional, never-ending, profound compassion. God longs for us to jettison the old destructive images of God and discover the truth of this love, Love with a capital 'L'. You have taken a step to do just that, by coming away on holiday with God. As you spend time with Jesus, becoming more open to the work of the Spirit, there is an invitation to trust God with more of the truth of who you are, even if that truth contains things you've kept hidden for a long time.

We all have a 'trust history' with highs and lows marking the way. When I think back over my own conscious 'trust in God' journey, which began seriously in my thirties, I remember leaning on God for the courage needed to take a funeral for the first time. A 32-year-old man, from a workplace where I was chaplain, had died of cancer. I recall arriving early at the church, watching the mainly male congregation assemble, and wondering nervously how what I had prepared might comfort and encourage those who were grieving. As the service began, however, a deep sense of peace settled around me like a soft blanket, and my anxieties melted away. Feedback later assured me that people were touched by the love of God in a time of pain.

God provided what I needed for that difficult task, and that experience became a waymarker on my 'trust' journey, a tangible example of God's grace being 'sufficient' in all circumstances when I acknowledge my 'weakness', my need of God (2 Corinthians 12.9).

Other 'trust in God' waymarkers have followed; some of them are simple but sparkling in the midst of daily detail, such as choosing the right card for my uncle's 81st birthday. Always a comedian, he was tickled when I sent him *two* cards – one for a 60 year old and the other for a 21 year old! An example of God's sense of humour at work! Other waymarkers are major, such as the birth of our son after years of infertility and, 12 years later, taking a year's leave to study in the UK and finding God trustworthy for finance, housing, work, schooling, the demands of full-time study, and the emotional wellbeing of my needy elderly mother.

God delights in being part of our lives and constantly provides opportunities to hone our trust skills. Our ability to take these opportunities grows as our relationship with God deepens, as we take each step in faith. We see this process illustrated in Peter. A fledgling awareness of the uniqueness of Jesus encouraged Peter to risk saying 'yes' and begin his own growth in Christ, even if it meant ignoring common sense and risking embarrassment. The three-year, daily journey with Jesus brought Peter to the point of confessing Jesus as the 'Christ, the son of the living God' (Matthew 16.16). But then Peter went through his own 'crucifixion': his self-image was shattered when he denied Jesus three times and was confronted by his cowardice. However, after the resurrection, again at the lake's edge, Jesus gives Peter the chance to affirm his commitment to Christ (John 21.3–14), and it is at this point, as the relationship with Jesus is being re-established, that Peter receives Jesus' commission to 'feed my sheep' (John 21.15–18). As we see in the book of Acts, opportunities to trust God more and more came thick and fast for Peter from that point. He was indeed venturing into those 'deep waters' to which Jesus had invited him at the start of his journey of trust.

While few of us are called to the intensity of Peter's experiences, we are all drawn towards a deeper giving of ourselves to the God who loves us beyond all understanding. As we gradually develop enough of a relationship to begin to put our lives into the hands of Jesus; as we come to *know* Jesus, rather than knowing about him, we are given the confidence we need to trust him with whatever life holds. Ultimately we will come to know, somewhere deep within, that we are truly, deeply beloved of God, and, in Julian of Norwich's words, 'All shall be well, and all shall be well, and all manner of things shall be well.'[8]

Deepening

✠ Where are you on your journey of learning to trust God?

Try drawing a timeline from birth to now, and use colour, words and symbols to represent key 'waymarkers' on your 'trust-in-God' journey.

✠ Has there been a time when you have trusted God but have felt let down?

Talk to God or Jesus about this as honestly as you can – even if it is difficult and you get angry or upset. Or write a letter to God about the circumstances … you can put it in your journal or shred or burn it later – your choice.

✠ What is your trust history with other people?

If you have ever betrayed someone, consider bringing that situation to God. Be assured that your God is with you as you remember and confess. Listen to God for guidance about reconciliation or some form of redress. When you have finished, take a cup of water, go outside, slowly pour the water onto the ground. As the water is absorbed into the earth, know that God absorbs your pain and guilt. You are free.

---

8 *Daily Readings with Julian of Norwich*, 1980, Darton, Longman & Todd, p. 15.

Closing prayer

Companion God, take me by the hand
and lead me to the place of trust
which waits for me in you.

You know my heart,
and all that clings to old hurts.
You know my mind,
and all that ruins my peace.
Enable me to let go of unholy habits,
and to welcome with joy your surprises and love.
May I become a bringer of light and a maker of peace
wherever you put me, whatever I do.

I make this prayer through Jesus
who trusted you, O God,
and weathered the wondering
of your presence, your absence
in the midst of his suffering.
Because of his death, because of his life,
I am blessed.
AMEN

On holiday with God

Waiting – *learning to 'be still'*

Focus verse

'Be still, and know that I am God!' (Psalm 46.10)

Opening prayer

Dear God,
I struggle with stillness
I am addicted to action
I am impatient for growth in grace,
   for freedom from fear;
   for more of your compassionate love.
To receive from you, I must learn to wait.
Your timing has the eternal in mind;
my timing is more of a daily battle
with hours and appointments and chores,
busyness gets in the way of simply being.
Help me dear God, to be still in you,
so I may know, and be known, in your Love.
AMEN

Scripture to use for lectio divina *or imaginative prayer*

[36]'And now, your relative Elizabeth in her old age has also conceived a son; and this is the sixth month for her who was said to be barren. [37]For nothing will be impossible with God.' [38]Then Mary said, 'Here am I, the servant of the LORD; let it be with me according to your word.' Then the angel departed from her.

[39]In those days Mary set out and went with great haste to a Judean town in the hill country, [40]where she entered the house of Zechariah and greeted Elizabeth. [41]When Elizabeth heard Mary's greeting, the child leaped in her womb. And Elizabeth was filled with the Holy Spirit [42] and exclaimed with a loud cry, 'Blessed are you among women, and blessed is the fruit of your womb. [43]And why has this happened to me, that the mother of my Lord

comes to me? [44]For as soon as I heard the sound of your greeting, the child in my womb leaped for joy. [45]And blessed is she who believed that there would be a fulfilment of what was spoken to her by the Lord.' ...

[56]And Mary remained with her about three months and then returned to her home.
(Luke 1.36–45, 56)

Personal reflection

ᗺ What has stirred within me as I have prayed this passage?

ᗺ With which woman do I identify more easily?

Further food for thought

Waiting may frustrate us, yet it is a common part of any holiday: waiting at airports, waiting in queues at art galleries or museums, waiting for service at restaurants. Waiting is part of your holiday time with God too, but this waiting has a different quality. This 'anointed' waiting, unique to retreat time, creates a climate of intense availability to the Spirit, in which your relationship with God can grow and inner change becomes possible.

But learning to be still is not easy. I don't know about you, but when I have to wait for any length of time, the urge to find something to *do* surfaces, unbidden. In a culture preoccupied with productivity, it's not surprising that the value of simply *being* is called into question, potentially sabotaging our attempts to be open to the movement of God in the stillness.

Most of us are used to waiting for things like test results (medical and academic), for the rain to pass, for a contemplative toddler exploring a flower, for a reply to a text message, email or letter. But there are times when waiting is especially hard. One example of hard waiting is infertility with its hidden sorrow, its chronic grief. Behind closed doors, the issue of blood is a monthly reminder of what is not to be. Longing for parenthood, women and men get on with their lives, awkward around family with new babies, angry with the careless who conceive without thought, waiting for costly IVF embryos to 'take' or for the rare opportunity to adopt. They wait and keep hoping until all possible options are exhausted, and childlessness becomes their reality.

Modern science can sometimes establish reasons for infertility, but in Elizabeth's time, it was the woman who bore the burden and shame of 'barrenness'. Elizabeth had waited. For years she had watched others bear and rear children and longed for her own. In her ageing, she would have moved beyond waiting, would have let go of the possibility and pleasure of motherhood, until God did the impossible, and miraculously touched the mature couple with the gift of a child.

Once her pregnancy was safely established, Elizabeth must have thought that nothing more wonderful could happen to her. Certainly she had to endure the silence of her husband, rendered mute by the affronted Gabriel for not believing such a blessing could be possible. But she was free to enjoy a period of anointed waiting, anticipating the joy that was to come with the birth of her special child. She was invited to that place of pure being, when the body is nurturing new life, and her part in that becoming was to rest and appreciate the unique child coming to fullness within her.

Then, in that place of deep contentment, something even more wonderful *does* happen: Mary calls her greeting and, immediately, the child in Elizabeth's womb 'leaps for joy' in ecstatic recognition of the presence of the tiny, true God-with-us in Mary's womb. Elizabeth, filled with the Spirit, is given a word of knowledge and can say with awestruck certainty that 'the mother of my Lord' has come to her. Mary too is overwhelmed by this encounter, as she experiences for herself the lively evidence of Elizabeth's pregnancy and greeting. The child forming within Mary's womb would be as extra-ordinary as any beloved human child, but also a unique expression of the presence of God. She is reassured that Gabriel's words to her ring with truth and she gives voice to her joy in the words that we know as the *Magnificat*: 'My soul magnifies the Lord ...' (Luke 1.46–55).

Mary and Elizabeth were being asked to be key players in God's mission to humanity, and so they needed unmistakable experiences of the grace and reality of God. Mothering John and Jesus would test these women. In the years ahead, reflecting on the moment of their meeting would strengthen them both, and remind them of God's call on their lives.

God entered the lives of both these women with amazing clarity, purpose and power, and as a result, their relationship with God took on new immediacy and richness. For most of us, however, growing in our relationship with God unfolds less dramatically. We can be slow to realize how much God loves us, or to appreciate the uniqueness of Jesus and his work on the cross. We are often frustrated at the frailty of our will, at the way we keep stumbling over the same faults. Our formation in holiness is hindered by weakness, laziness, comfort-seeking and self-doubt (these are some of my particular flaws – feel free to replace with your own!). Time and again we turn to God, disappointed when we don't make the 'progress' we think we should, as we seek to become as Christ to our families and community. Yet God still welcomes us, helps us start over, reassures us of a continuing love and provision for us, if only we have eyes to see, and ears to hear.

You might have come on holiday with God with expectations of some holy moments, some encounter, or special experience of God's presence. You may have heard of other people for whom God has 'turned up' in some mystical way and you hope that will happen to you. Perhaps you are, even now, getting a bit fed up with *waiting for 'something'* to happen.

The good news is that 'something' has already happened. You are here. You are *waiting for a 'someone'*, not for an idea, a new insight or a peak experience, but a *person* – for God, for the Compassionate One. If God had not already touched your heart, you would not be reading this book; you would not have made the effort to take time to be with God alone. This desire is the work of the Holy Spirit in your heart. God is already present to you, relating to you – through your inner awareness, through creation, through Scripture, through 'God-incidences', through people who love you, through children and pets, through music and singing, through art and architecture ...

And God is waiting for you now:
like a lover at a railway station – with passion
like a child awake on Christmas Eve – with playful anticipation
like a dear friend with the coffee brewing – with patience.

Waiting – learning to 'be still'

God is waiting for you – now – isn't that good news?
All you have to do now is to open your heart to that reality
and, in turn, wait upon God, who is Love.

Deepening

✠ Write your own *Magnificat* of thanksgiving and praise.

✠ Prayerfully reflect on your experiences of 'waiting' – both the hard times and the joyful times. What did you learn about yourself, about your God?

✠ Take 10–15 minutes to begin to practise centring prayer.

Relax, breathe easily, and gently repeat a sacred word such as 'Jesus', 'abide' or 'Maranatha' (Come, LORD Jesus) to serve as an anchor while you open your spirit to the Spirit of God. When distractions come, simply turn your mind back to your anchor word, as a sign of your intention to be fully available to God.

✠ Spend some time with the picture of the meeting of Mary and Elizabeth which was at the start of this retreat theme.

Closing prayer

Ever-faithful God,
In your word I read that
'… those who wait for the LORD
shall renew their strength,
they shall mount up with wings like eagles,
they shall run and not be weary,
they shall walk and not faint.' (Isaiah 40.31)
Bring strength to my own times of waiting,
when the way forward is uncertain
and hope seems distant.
Help me to wait for you, daily,
in delightful expectation that
you are waiting for me too. AMEN

On holiday with God

In the marketplace – *setting priorities*

Focus verse

Choose life so that you and your descendants may live, loving the LORD your God, obeying him, and holding fast to him; for that means life to you and length of days ... (Deuteronomy 30.19b–20a).

Opening prayer

Holy God, full of grace and wisdom,
help me to make you my priority,
in spite of the pull and attraction of so much
that distracts me from
your way and your will.
AMEN

Scripture to use for lectio divina *or imaginative prayer*

13The Passover of the Jews was near, and Jesus went up to Jerusalem. 14In the temple he found people selling cattle, sheep and doves, and the money-changers seated at their tables. 15Making a whip of cords, he drove all of them out of the temple, both the sheep and the cattle. He also poured out the coins of the money-changers and overturned their tables. 16He told those who were selling the doves, 'Take these things out of here! Stop making my Father's house a marketplace!'
(John 2.13–16)

Personal reflection

   How does this picture of Jesus compare with the image of 'gentle Jesus, meek and mild' whom you may have encountered in childhood?

   What aspect of this story touches your heart or mind?

Further food for thought

Wherever you've travelled, you've probably spent time in local markets. With their kaleidoscoping colours, exotic aromas, unfamiliar foods and narrow aisles packed with goods both tasteful and tawdry, markets can be full of surprising discoveries about a different way of life. It's fun to find a bargain or a beautiful and distinctive reminder of the place we are visiting, or a gift for someone special. Even if we return home and sigh at the silliness of some of our choices, we can smile at the memory and share the story freely.

But if we have the opportunity to go beneath the surface and talk to some of the market-stall holders, in spite of limited shared vocabulary, behind the bright facade we may glimpse something more concerning: stories of exploitation, of deprivation and great hardship. I recall seeing Bedouin families, living in ramshackle dwellings, deprived of their traditional nomadic lifestyle, eking out a living by selling hand-made jewellery; children making rugs in dark and dingy conditions in Egypt; and ageing merchants in the Old City of Jerusalem trying to get the small numbers of tourists to buy their wares, their desperation almost tangible. There are similar stories to be heard in markets anywhere, as the *anawim*[9] try to make ends meet. If we share these stories when we return home, it is with sorrow and a sense of helplessness; and perhaps, for a little while, we take more notice of how and where we spend our money.

There is another dimension operating in marketplaces all over the world too: the layer of the shrewd operator who makes a more

---

9 *Anawim* (Hebrew), 'the poor seeking God for deliverance', e.g. Psalm 37.11: 'Blessed are the *anawim* for they shall inherit the earth.'

than adequate living by overcharging and underhand dealing. Behind the scenes, away from the understanding of most casual tourists, lie systems and networks that indulge greed and self-seeking. We can be totally unaware of such a dimension unless we get home and realize we have been 'ripped off', and then the stories we tell are of anger and frustration and disappointment which can taint the whole experience and work against the poor caught in the subsistence nightmare.

In the time of Jesus, commerce had insinuated itself closer to the sanctuary of God; the outer courts of the Temple had become a marketplace: a bustling, noisy, smelly assortment of animals for sacrifice, their vendors and the pilgrims or penitents who were anxious to reach their destination, the inner court, as close as they could get to the Temple itself. Power in this 'marketplace' lay with the priests and the money-changers. In Jesus' time people were expected to pay an annual temple tax in only one currency – the Hebrew half-shekel. Jews coming to the Temple with the wrong coins or travellers with foreign currency had to deal with the money-changers, who set exorbitant rates of exchange, controlling access to the required half-shekel as well as changing money for those who wanted to buy sacrificial animals or birds, sold at inflated prices. Religious leaders turned a blind eye to the unjust practices, and were complicit with the money-changers in hindering access to God's holy places.

No wonder Jesus was furious! Instead of people leaving the Temple to return home to talk of being awed by the grace of the moment they had entered God's earthly courts, their stories might well have included accounts of exploitation as they were caught up in the marketplace's greed. The Temple had become an obstacle instead of a gateway to God. Jesus, in his interruption of temple commerce, was pointing towards the time when the way to God would be fully accessible through Jesus himself, and the Temple would 'cease trading' altogether, destroyed totally by the Romans in 70 AD.

As we draw closer to God, as we grow into the likeness of Christ, we are confronted by *our* attitudes towards other people, the way we use *our* authority or power, the ethics of *our* business practices, and the prejudices and preferences that shape *our* choices. God will invite us to look at our attitudes to money, the choices we make with our resources, and how we set our priorities. Sometimes a review of such fundamental aspects of our lives will bring us into conflict with others, sometimes it will provoke a personal, inner struggle as we seek to reconcile what we know of the call of God to justice and generosity with a lifestyle that is comfortable, even complacent.

If we live in the West, we face a deluge of distraction from media, marketing and materialism. However, if we are serious about making Godly choices, if we truly want to live lightly on the planet, if we want to reduce toxic influences and share our resources with those less fortunate, then we will need to practise prayerful discernment about:

- ॐ what we buy
- ॐ what we listen to or watch
- ॐ to whom or what we give our allegiance
- ॐ how we share our resources and abilities
- ॐ how we care for our planet
- ॐ how we connect with the wider community
- ॐ whom we welcome into our home
- ॐ how we dispose of our assets after our death.

It may seem hard work to begin to change our way of acting in the marketplace, and even harder to influence the 'big players' in industries such as tobacco and alcohol. But we *can* make a difference if we begin with our own sphere of influence and then see where God might lead us. Perhaps God is inviting you to be part of the dismantling of something that hinders the flowing of abundant life which God desires for all humankind. If so, God *will* guide, equip and enable you to be part of the solution rather than part of the problem.

We've been considering setting priorities in our outward life of work, resource management, leisure and so on. But we also need to consider our priorities in relation to our spiritual life. A friend recently shared a memory of getting off a train in a busy overseas location and being almost bowled over by the maelstrom of humanity surging around her. She had to pull herself back onto the train so she could pause and prepare herself for this new environment. As she reflected later, that experience reminded her how important it was to step back from the mad rush of life, so she could catch her breath with God and *be resourced spiritually* for what lay ahead.

Keeping close to God in daily prayer, being alert for the 'nudges' of the Spirit, regular 'interior glances' towards the God who is present in the quiet centre of our soul, letting words of Scripture or glimpses of beauty from the creation 're-mind' us of the ways of God and the life and example of Jesus, all help to develop and maintain a strong spiritual connection with God. This spiritual resourcing not only settles our focus firmly on the things of God, but provides a reference point against which our decisions about consumption, acquisition or disposal of goods can be measured.

If we truly want to live a simple life, unencumbered by what most of western society promotes as necessary, we shall be challenged. We can only meet that challenge if we are standing on the solid ground of a strong vibrant relationship with God, 'in whose service is perfect freedom' and bubbling joy!

Deepening

✠ How have you been helped or hindered on your journey of faith in the past? Bring to God any painful memories of abuse of power in the context of church participation. Give thanks to God for those who have been mentors or spiritual parents over the years.

✠ Make a pie-graph to get an idea of where your resources of time and money are currently distributed. Talk to God about your responsibilities and the wisdom of your choices.

✠ How do you behave 'in the marketplace' of contemporary life in relation to ethical practices, honesty and fairness?

✠ How can you make time to be with God in prayer a priority in the midst of the busy marketplace of life?

Closing prayer

Jesus,
you know what I have and what I currently do with it.
You know the needs of my family, and my neighbourhood
and the part I already play in filling those needs.
But you also know that I want to be wise in my spending
of money, of time, of skills and of energy.
Help me to make choices that will
bring life to those around me;
help me to look beyond my own community
to the world you love so very much;
remind me to step aside from the busyness so
I can draw deeply from your love
and better serve your kingdom.
AMEN

On holiday with God

On the water – *dealing with fear*

Focus verse

So do not fear, for I am with you;
do not be dismayed, for I am your God.
I will strengthen you and help you;
I will uphold you with my righteous right hand.
(Isaiah 41.10)

Opening prayer

Dear God,
you know my 'fear' history,
the times when I have been weighed down
with worry, the times when I have struggled alone.
How often you have been waiting to help me,
but I did not invite you into my reality,
and so I missed the solace of your Spirit
and the comfort of your peace.
Help me today to find a new way of dealing with fear,
through your Son, my brother Jesus.
AMEN

Scripture to use for lectio divina *or imaginative prayer*

²²Immediately he made the disciples get into the boat and go on ahead to the other side, while he dismissed the crowds. ²³And after he had dismissed the crowds, he went up the mountain by himself to pray. When evening came, he was there alone, ²⁴but by this time the boat, battered by the waves, was far from the land, for the wind was against them. ²⁵And early in the morning he came walking towards them on the lake. ²⁶But when the disciples saw him walking on the lake, they were terrified, saying, 'It is a ghost!' And they cried out in fear. ²⁷But immediately Jesus spoke to them and said, 'Take heart, it is I; do not be afraid.'

²⁸Peter answered him, 'Lord, if it is you, command me to come to you on the water.' ²⁹He said, 'Come.' So Peter got out of the boat, started walking on the water, and came towards Jesus. ³⁰But when he noticed the strong wind, he became frightened, and beginning to sink, he cried out, 'Lord, save me!' ³¹Jesus immediately reached out his hand and caught him, saying to him, 'You of little faith, why did you doubt?' ³²When they got into the boat, the wind ceased. ³³And those in the boat worshipped him, saying, 'Truly you are the Son of God.'
(Matthew 14.22–33)

Personal reflection

ĝ   What word or phrase has spoken to you today?

ĝ   What might this passage say to you about your own fearfulness?

Further food for thought

In this section focusing on dealing with fear, I am not thinking of people with deep-seated neuroses or psychiatric conditions that require specialist diagnosis and treatment. I am thinking about those of us who function well on a day-to-day basis, but who worry a lot or get caught up in fear and anxiety, and risk missing out on the freedom and lightness of living which God intended.

When we go away on holiday to our cottage at Lake Taupo in the summer, a residue of fear goes with me because of my history with water and boating. So whenever we go out on this large lake, which, like the Sea of Galilee can chop up quickly in high winds and produce metre high swells without much warning, I actively invite Jesus to be with me. I picture him beside me in the boat WIDE AWAKE – not sleeping in the warm cabin below away from the effects of the wind and cold. Several times I've had to hold his hand – in my imagination, but still real enough for me – as we have bounced our way safely back to the marina. It's taken me a long time to get to this point of 'feeling the fear but doing it *any* way', and my way is to invite Jesus into the picture and to lean heavily on him.

The frequent appearance of the words 'Do not be afraid' in the Bible is no accident, but an acknowledgement that fear is a reality for humanity. Yet for those of us who have been taught that we 'shouldn't' feel worried or anxious about anything because Christ 'gives us the victory', a burden of guilt and failure is added to an already struggling faith. So it is important to say from the beginning that just having a fearful thought or a worrying idea is not a failure of faith. It is simply a reminder that you are human, still journeying towards the 'perfection in love' Christ offers:

> There is no fear in love, but perfect love casts out fear; for fear has to do with punishment, and whoever fears has not reached perfection in love.
> (1 John 4.18)

We are created with the capacity to feel emotion, mediated through our particular temperament and interpreted by our personal life experience. For many of us this unique personhood means that, even though we are getting to know our God day by day; even though we might sense the companioning Presence of Christ; even though the Spirit is a real Comforter, we still feel fearful or anxious some times because that's simply how we are made. It is not a sin to have a worrying thought – it is what we do with those thoughts that may or may not lead us into sin, and by sin I mean whatever separates us from God. We can choose whether fear drives us further from God like a tornado of anxiety gathering momentum and blocking out the Light, or whether fear makes us run to the shelter of those everlasting arms, to the safety of our brother Jesus who can calm any storm we are ever likely to face.

It is all too easy to get into a 'habit' of fear – like literally waking up in the morning and putting on a garment that hampers our freedom and limits our lightness of living. There are plenty of things that we could be afraid *for*: our children's futures, the state of the global economy, the place of the church in local and public life. And there are plenty of things to be afraid *of*: failing financially, getting cancer, being found out over something we've done or not done; growing old, being lonely, falling out with friends, losing our mind, death itself ... But we have a choice: we can lurch from fear to fear on our own, or we can face each day letting God deal with our fears with us, for us.

If we stop long enough to look at what we fear, we can see that many of our fears lie in an unknowable future. To live the abundant life which God offers us, we cannot spend time being afraid of what might never happen, nor can we try to 'second-guess' what might be best in a situation and then agonize when things don't run according to our plans. I spent years shaping my life around my mother's emotional needs, and it was only when God showed me (while I was on retreat) my deep-seated fear of her anger and disapproval, that I was able to step back, stop trying to make her happy, and really let her go into God's care. In the years before her death I saw God at work in her life – a kind Christian neighbour mentored her, older friends welcomed her into their group and she came to a level of self-acceptance and contentment that had seemed impossible.

I did not have to make it happen – *God* did the work of grace.

You don't have to *solve* apparently intransigent situations which cause you fear and anxiety – your part is to hold those people and situations before God in prayer, trusting that God will be at work and will somehow, in God's time, bring difficult situations to resolution and draw those for whom you pray ever closer to healing and wholeness.

So, if you are a 'worrier', then 'take heart', as Jesus says. With the help of the Comforter, the Holy Spirit, you *can* make a change in how you react to fear in your life by prayerfully bringing your worries and fears to God *as soon as* you experience anxious thoughts or that sinking feeling in your stomach. Instead of 'entertaining' a fear so it magnifies and threatens to overwhelm you, 'take every thought captive to obey Christ' (2 Corinthians 10.5b). Disarm the fear by shining the Light of Christ on it. Together with Jesus, look at it from every angle so that fear has no secrets and can hold no power over you. With the guidance of the Holy Spirit, spend time in quiet prayer until you get a clear idea of the fear and its layers so you can name them before God. What do I mean by 'layers'? Say, for example, that I am anxious about how people might take what I have to say in my sermon on Sunday. That's a legitimate and understandable fear of rejection and failure, but there is another layer to the situation – behind that fear is my greater fear that I might let God down and somehow disgrace my priestly vocation.

To deal effectively with fear, we need to be as honest as we can about what we are *really* afraid of, before God. Every time we name and 'capture' our fears in this way, it's like putting up a STOP sign so the anxious 'train of thought' cannot proceed. Instead our mind can move to the words of Paul in Philippians 4.6–7:

> Do not worry about anything, but in everything by prayer and supplication with thanksgiving let your requests be made known to God. And the peace of God, which surpasses all understanding, will guard your hearts and your minds in Christ Jesus.

This conversion in your thinking may take time, but as the practice becomes familiar, you will begin to know the 'stop sign' strategy is working when the clamour of the voice of fear is quietened, and the soothing words of Scripture and the calming tones of the Spirit touch and strengthen your being.

Our God *encourages* us in times of need. At the centre of 'encouragement' is *cor* – the Latin word for **heart** and **daring**. The Bible is full of God's desire for us to be fearless, and brave; to live with a minimum of fear and anxiety and a greater measure of care for others. 'Take heart', Jesus says to the frightened disciples in the storm. Into the darkness of their fear, our fear, Christ comes, helping us face any fear we are willing to name and bring to him. But if we pretend that we've got it all together, if we think we are self-sufficient, if we believe that God's got far too much to deal with or that our needs are too small to be of interest to the great God of the Universe, we deny ourselves the very help that *does* make a difference even in the darkest of moments.

Peter – even if it was an act of bravado – was able to put aside his fears, climb over the edge of the boat, and begin to walk towards Jesus. For just a few moments he experienced the absolute fearlessness that lightens us – physically, emotionally, spiritually – when we fix our eyes totally on Jesus. But fear sneaked into Peter's mind and weighed him down, just as it does with us whenever we take our eyes off our Lord. Keep your eyes on Jesus and fear begins to fade. As I heard in a recent sermon:

'Don't worry,' says Jesus, 'it's okay. It's me. I am here.'[10]
And he is – always has been, is now, and always will be. Forever.

Deepening

✠ Spend some time quietly reflecting on any current fears. Name these fears before God, as honestly as you can.

✠ Pray with the words of Paul in Philippians 4.6–7

✠ It's not uncommon for people to be afraid of God. If you feel that way, don't panic. Bring this fear to Jesus, as friend and brother. Talk to him about it as much as you can and let him, when the time is right, bring you to God who waits for you as Welcomer, as Kindness itself.

Closing prayer

Loving God, you tell us that 'perfect love casts out fear'.
Help me to make space in my heart for more of your love,
so my mind may be freed from futile fear
and may focus instead on you.
Teach me each day to turn to you
whenever worries threaten to invade my peace.
For in you my life is kept safe, my mind is kept sound.
Thank you, O God of love. AMEN

---

10 Quoted from a sermon by the Revd Harry Hicks, Rotorua, New Zealand 7.8.11.

On holiday with God

Gallery or garden – *appreciating beauty*

Focus verse

He hath sent me ... unto them that mourn in Zion,
to give unto them beauty for ashes,
the oil of joy for mourning,
the garment of praise for the spirit of heaviness ...
(Isaiah 61.1b, 3a King James)

Opening prayer

Creator God,
today I look across to a sea
bluer than the iris flowers
unfolding in my garden,
and I wonder at your world
and the beauty of it all –
from the simplest organism
to the farthest galaxy,
shimmering colours and vibrancy
fit for the fireworks of a king.
But there is other beauty too,
that you want me to see,
not so noticeable,
shy even,
and part of that beauty
is me.
Help me to notice my own beauty
amidst the shadows of my life.
AMEN

Scripture to use for lectio divina *or imaginative prayer*

[33]Then they came to Capernaum; and when he was in the house he asked them, 'What were you arguing about on the way?' [34]But they were silent, for on the way they had argued with one another who was the greatest. [35]He sat down, called the twelve, and said to them, 'Whoever wants to be first must be last of all and servant of all.' [36]Then he took a little child and put it among them; and taking it in his arms, he said to them, [37]'Whoever welcomes one such child in my name welcomes me, and whoever welcomes me welcomes not me but the one who sent me.'
(Mark 9.33–37)

Personal reflection

⸙ How do you view the disciples' squabbling over status?
How important is rank or position – and their benefits – to your sense of worth or wellbeing?

⸙ Imagine yourself as that little child being picked up by Jesus and brought into the centre of the adult conversation.
What is that like?
How do you feel?
What does Jesus say or do?

Further food for thought

Where do you go to find beauty?
To your mirror?
To the glossy magazine's carefully crafted photographs of houses built of marble and millions?
Do you go to gardens of note, mountain peaks, snow and sky, colours of birds and butterflies, expanse of plain and ocean, fragrance of herbs and roses, shapes and shadows of trees?
Or do you go, as many on holiday go, to theatres of music, dance or drama, to museums and art galleries where paintings and porcelain, sculpture and architecture make your spirit soar and rejoice at human creativity?

Gallery or garden – appreciating beauty

Where *do* you go to find beauty? It would seem that Jesus' disciples were thinking that beauty and attractiveness had something to do with status and its benefits. They were squabbling among themselves about who was 'most likely to succeed' in the discipleship stakes, measuring achievement by the conventions of the day, where having power over others was everything.

But the beauty of which the prophet writes, the beauty which Jesus embodies, is entirely different:

> How beautiful upon the mountains are the feet of the messenger who announces peace, who brings good news, who announces salvation, who says to Zion, 'Your God reigns.'
> (Isaiah 52.7)

Isaiah wrote to highlight the hope and promise of liberation for 'Zion', the Hebrew people whose long captivity in Babylon had rendered them powerless, disconnected from their roots and all that shaped their being. For them, hundreds of years before Christ, beauty was to be found in the bearer of that 'good news' of return to their homeland. For the disciples of Jesus, their beauty would be found not in power-seeking but in sharing the stories of Jesus, in encouraging those who felt exiled from hope during the Roman occupation of Palestine to know that another more enduring kingdom, the kingdom of God was, in Jesus, within reach.

The writer of the psalms sees beauty as an attribute of God:

> One thing I asked of the LORD, that will I seek after:
> to live in the house of the LORD all the days of my life,
> to behold the beauty of the LORD, and
> to inquire in his temple. (Psalm 27.4)

and

> Worship the LORD in the beauty of holiness ... (Psalm 29.2)

The psalmist draws us closer to the true meaning of beauty, pointing us towards holiness, purity, grace and welcome, towards the fruits of the Spirit (Galatians 5.22–23) given flesh and form in Jesus, birthed from the fullness of God.

Jesus finds an example of this understanding of beauty in a little child. Trying to transform his disciples' self-interest into an understanding of what the Kingdom of God requires of them, Jesus picks a child up and draws their attention to this little one who has no status or power whatsoever. Under Egyptian dominance in the time of Moses, and under Roman oppression in the time of Jesus, Hebrew children were expendable in the eyes of those with political or military power. But to Jesus, this child is a symbol of the love of God, and of the way of Jesus, which is the way of simplicity, vulnerability and humility, not the way of status-seeking or the wilful exercise of authority over others.

Only yesterday, sitting at the early morning Eucharist, I found myself looking into the eyes of a little boy whose mum – as mothers among us can understand – had just managed to get to church with him, halfway through the service. He was about seven or eight months old, with a lovely sturdy back and strong body, hands seeking things to explore, eyes widely scanning the new environment. His mum tried to keep track of the service while holding him on her knee, and occasionally giving a quiet 'Sssh' as he murmured to her or chuckled to himself. Babies are natural contemplatives, so when he looked across at me, he was not hurried, nor did his gaze slide away after a cursory glance. He steadily considered me and I settled my gaze on him in response. He was not a 'beautiful' child, his nose was a bit runny and his cheeks were a bit grubby, but that didn't matter. There was a smile, and with it a whole depth of potential and unexpected wisdom and gentle kindness in those eyes that touched my heart. In him the beauty of God was made visible, yet again, in the miracle of ongoing incarnation.

This little boy was beautiful to me; the child in the Gospel story was beautiful to Jesus. Both of them, still fragrant with the Love from whom they have come, are messengers of God to help us see what really matters: welcome and wonder, openness and trust, connection and confidence, and being vehicles of grace to those around us, rather than using others to fulfil our own projects or cravings for power.

Gallery or garden – appreciating beauty

Beauty in our twenty-first-century western context is often linked to the superficial, transitory or contrived looks of the 'famous' and the wealthy. Jesus, however, was clear about the difference between the external impression someone gives and the interior disposition of the heart. He was scathing of those who looked good on the outside but were less than holy on the inside:

> Woe to you, scribes and Pharisees, hypocrites! For you are like whitewashed tombs, which on the outside look beautiful, but inside they are full of the bones of the dead and all kinds of filth. So you also on the outside look righteous to others, but inside you are full of hypocrisy and lawlessness.
> (Matthew 23.27–28)

Jesus seeks honesty not hypocrisy, even if being honest means being angry or disappointed or floundering in our faith. He encourages us to share our truth with him, even if we are uncertain, or in pain, or struggling to follow what we think is his call. Instead of pretending, we are asked to be upfront even if we are admitting to things of which we are ashamed. Jesus' disciples were embarrassed to tell him of their dispute, but Jesus knew what was going on, just as he knows what is going on in our inner lives. We are frail, and wonderful, and irritating, and beautiful all at once – but Jesus knows that, deep down, we are turned *towards* him, that we long to be like him, despite our weaknesses.

In spite of their squabbling, those disciples centuries ago ultimately managed to be messengers of the good news of God's grace. So can we, praise God, because transformation is what Jesus offers. We need no longer be at the mercy of our circumstances or our moods, nor the fears that afflict our mind. Instead, we come to know that we stand in a safe, broad place with the Son of God beside us, and with a clear listening space within us, where the Spirit of Jesus can revive our spirit. Isaiah's words again speak poignantly of this transformation, his message directed at the people of God who were fearful and isolated, but just as relevant to all of us who feel that way today. For those who mourn in Zion, the anointed One of God will, Isaiah writes,

... give unto them beauty for ashes,
the oil of joy for mourning,
the garment of praise
for the spirit of heaviness;
that they might be called trees of righteousness,
the planting of the LORD,
that he might be glorified.
(Isaiah 61.3)

Jesus, the Anointed One of God, the Messiah, comes among us still, through the work of the Holy Spirit. He helps us begin to find beauty in unexpected places: in a bird at work in nest building; in the sky reflected in a puddle of rain; in a passage of Scripture that touches us unexpectedly. The Spirit helps us to find beauty in people whom we had thought ugly, in situations we had thought intractable, and perhaps most unexpectedly, in our own selves in spite of our sense of guilt or failure or inadequacy. Many of us carry the echo of critical adults' voices which still have the power to upset our sense of worth and personhood, but Jesus' voice is stronger than the voices of disapproval or fear. Like the little child placed in the circle of adults to help them learn about the true nature of servanthood, we are precious in Jesus' sight.

A life lived in love is beautiful even as a person approaches death. I am thinking of an old lady whom I will call Meg. She had limited energy but her sparkling eyes and radiant smile literally lightened her room. After she died, I heard person after person express gratitude for her love and the way she had made them feel special. The light of her love had touched so many that she epitomized Teresa of Calcutta's teaching about doing 'something beautiful for God', not something large or spectacular but something small and beautiful – and that is what Meg did – she saw us as beautiful, loved each person who came into her room and each of us knew she loved us, and was blessed.

Look in the mirror again and see yourself through God's eyes; know that you are beautiful; be blessed and be a blessing.

Gallery or garden – appreciating beauty

Deepening

✠ Consider one situation with which you currently struggle, and ask God to help you see a glimmer of grace, something beautiful that can be a message of hope for you, 'beauty for ashes'.

✠ Reflect on your faith journey and name those people or places which showed you something of the beauty of God.

✠ Make a collage to express something of your understanding of beauty.

✠ When you are back home, begin to look for the beauty hidden around you among family, friends, community.

Closing prayer

O Beautiful God,
holy and wise,
warm and welcoming,
sometimes I forget that
your image animates my life,
and pulses through my being.
Help me notice
the movements of your Spirit
towards all that is good and pure
and beautiful, so that
balance might return to my
topsy-turvy life,
and with it,
a sense of my own beauty.
For when I know that I am
beautiful in your sight,
then I will more easily see
the beauty in others.
AMEN

On holiday with God

Walking – *making a pilgrimage*

Focus verse

Blessed are those whose strength is in you,
who have set their hearts on pilgrimage.
(Psalm 84.5 NIV)

Opening prayer

Companion God,
I hear of others who have made a pilgrimage
to holy sites near and far.
I am on pilgrimage too –
it is a journey with peaks and valleys,
not smooth or straight or easy
as my heart learns to listen,
and my mind to understand
that you love me through and through.
Help me to notice your love
sprinkled through the day
like icing-sugar, sweetening
the sadness with your consolation,
dusting the details with your
delight in me.
Thank you O God
for going on pilgrimage with me
each day, all my days.
AMEN

Scripture to use for lectio divina *or imaginative prayer*

[13]Now on that same day two of them were going to a village called Emmaus, about seven miles from Jerusalem, [14]and talking with each other about all these things that had happened. [15]While they were talking and discussing, Jesus himself came near and went with them, [16]but their eyes were kept from recognizing him. [17]And

he said to them, 'What are you discussing with each other while you walk along?' They stood still, looking sad. [18]Then one of them, whose name was Cleopas, answered him, 'Are you the only stranger in Jerusalem who does not know the things that have taken place there in these days?' [19]He asked them, 'What things?' They replied, 'The things about Jesus of Nazareth, who was a prophet mighty in deed and word before God and all the people, [20]and how our chief priests and leaders handed him over to be condemned to death and crucified him. [21]But we had hoped that he was the one to redeem Israel. Yes, and besides all this, it is now the third day since these things took place. [22]Moreover, some women of our group astounded us. They were at the tomb early this morning, [23]and when they did not find his body there, they came back and told us that they had indeed seen a vision of angels who said that he was alive ...'

[25]Then he said to them, 'Oh, how foolish you are, and how slow of heart to believe all that the prophets have declared! [26]Was it not necessary that the Messiah should suffer these things and then enter into his glory?' [27]Then beginning with Moses and all the prophets, he interpreted to them the things about himself in all the scriptures.

[28]As they came near the village to which they were going, he walked ahead as if he were going on. [29]But they urged him strongly, saying, 'Stay with us, because it is almost evening and the day is now nearly over.' So he went in to stay with them. [30]When he was at the table with them, he took bread, blessed and broke it, and gave it to them. [31]Then their eyes were opened, and they recognized him; and he vanished from their sight. [32]They said to each other, 'Were not our hearts burning within us, while he was talking to us on the road, while he was opening the scriptures to us?' (Luke 24.13–23, 25–32)

Personal reflection

§ What moves you as you reflect on this scripture?

§ How has Jesus come alongside you on your life's journey? Did you discern his presence at the time or in hindsight?

Walking – making a pilgrimage

Further food for thought

When we are on retreat, walking becomes a contemplative practice which helps us to be open to God and to discover more about our motivation, values and inner life. Because we are moving at a pace that is natural, in harmony with our humanity, there's more time to think, to make unexpected discoveries along the way, more chances to step aside and stop if something intrigues us.

Making a pilgrimage on foot has long been a practice associated with the major faiths of the world. Whether the destination is Jerusalem or Mecca, Santiago de Compostela in northern Spain, Iona off west Scotland or Lindisfarne off north-east England, or less well-known, but locally significant sites around the globe, people are being drawn in increasing numbers to make a pilgrimage, seeking the sacred. But making a pilgrimage is not an easy option. It requires energy, time, resources, courage and a willingness to have our hearts and minds – and bodies – tested as never before.

What moves us to make such an effort? Although a few people may make these journeys simply out of curiosity or to keep a friend company, for most it is a search for something more meaningful and solid than the western distractions of retail 'therapy', 24/7 entertainment, social networking, glamorous travel destinations, casual relationships and uncertain futures; a search for something that will satisfy our hungry souls. St Augustine left us these words which resonate with those who go on pilgrimage:

(O God) 'thou hast made us for thyself and restless is our heart until it comes to rest in thee'.[11]

This profound restlessness stems from our longing for a deeper sense of connection with the God who created us. We are born for that relationship, it is as natural as breathing, and just as vital. Making a pilgrimage provides a context in which we can address this longing, and experience both community connection and personal discovery. As that 'I – Thou' search deepens and begins to come alive, we find ourselves reaching *outwards* to other people and our world, and reaching *within* to accept our inner reality, our needs and dreams.

---

11 Augustine of Hippo, *Confessions*, Book 1, Chapter 1.

When pilgrims deliberately give away the hectic pace and com-
forts of home in favour of simpler, reflective 'time out', shared
with like-minded people from around the world, they find themselves immersed in the mystery of God. By walking together and
helping each other to reach a common goal, they catch a glimpse
of the body of Christ, with all its diversity and camaraderie, struggles and achievements. Community develops as connections are
made through the shared stories, the mutual support offered, the
singing and the companionable silence; self-awareness increases
as pilgrims pay attention to their own thoughts and feelings, make
the daily, deep connection with creation, and allow the layers
of roles, work, country, age, denomination and gender to take
second place to the reality of shared humanity.

And that was what it was like for Jesus and his disciples. He
conducted his ministry slowly, on foot most of the time, apart
from the occasional use of a boat or a donkey. Jesus moved at a
pace that allowed people to be close to him, to join him on the
journey, to sit and rest with him, to eat with him, to be touched
by his healing and warmed by his very being.

One of the most detailed accounts of a journey with Jesus is
in this Gospel. Two people, walking away from the horror of
Golgotha and the dashed hopes of deliverance, are met unexpectedly by a 'stranger'. Preoccupied, grieving, stunned and sad, it's
not surprising that they did not immediately recognize Jesus. He,
in turn, chooses not to identify himself immediately, giving them
time to allow their feelings and thoughts to come to the surface
while he listens. It is only when they have had the chance to share
their story that he begins to reveal something about himself. Beginning with the scriptural record of his presence woven through the
Law and the Prophets, and ending with the re-membering of the
meal shared with his disciples at Passover, Jesus reveals to the disciples the present miraculous reality that here is the Risen Christ,
in his resurrection body. With them, as with us, he is known to
them 'in the breaking of the bread', sharing himself with the whole
of humanity in eternal Eucharistic communion.

As it was for these disciples, one of the hardest times in our
life pilgrimage is when we suffer a great loss – the death of someone we love. At that time, unless we receive wise companionship,

we may not recognize the Christ who walks with us through the long hard valley of the shadow. Worse still, we may turn against the God whom we may have known before and, with profound but often unexpressed anger blurring our vision, declare that God impotent and unjust – or dead too. Some of you reading this book may have been on that hardest of journeys and perhaps, wondering where God was when this dreadful loss darkened your life, you cried Jesus' words:

'My God, my God, why have you forsaken me?'
(Mark 15.34)

Jesus made his pilgrimage all the way to the cross and its appalling sense of God's abandonment. That's what Jesus in his humanity felt – and yet he still chose not to 'Curse God, and die', as Job's wife suggested to her husband in his abject distress (Job 2.9), but to turn his face towards his Father in a final act of trust:

'Father, into your hands I commend my spirit.'
(Luke 23.46)

This is what Jesus revealed to those with him in the 'breaking of the bread': that in spite of their feelings, in spite of their trauma, in spite of their disappointment and the failed hopes and dreams, Jesus' pilgrimage did not end at the tomb. Death is not the end. Resurrection life awaited him, and awaits us. He is alive and available to you and to me as we journey, whenever we stop long enough to pay attention to what is happening in our inner life, when we notice that 'our hearts burn within us' and recognize the indwelling presence of the Spirit of Jesus working with our spirit to bring healing and hopefulness. God still holds the whole earth in tender hands, and Love is stronger than any death.

Some of you may not have directly experienced the loss of someone close to you, but you may have friends or extended family members who have, and you may have wondered how to be with them in their numb silence or in their white-hot rage turned inwards in depression or outwards in destructive behaviours. Be guided by Jesus' way of being with these two disorientated disciples: be an attentive listener, a respectful presence, a patient fellow traveller, keeping your friend company until the opportunity opens for 'sitting down together', for breaking of bread and, if you can, for helping them notice the small mercies that are signs of God's provision, faithfulness and presence. Those mercies will be there in the care and love of those around them, in the details of daily living, if their eyes are opened to see them.

Your pilgrimage of faith may have encountered many ups and downs, moments of absolute conviction and muddled times of doubt and wandering. But you are here, now, and Jesus is sitting with you as you read these words, helping you through his Spirit, to notice God's presence around and within you. As you have journeyed to this place of retreat you have joined the countless people from many faiths who have made their way to a sacred place in order to deepen their relationship with God. Although, for this particular pilgrimage, you may not have travelling companions who are visible and actively part of your experience, nevertheless you bring with you – in faith and memory – all those who have contributed to your spiritual journey to this point. And you make your retreat with the support of those who pray for you at home, and in the sight of the community of the faithful who have gone before you.

As you allow God to walk with you into areas of your life that are full of tension or sadness, into rooms in your soul that are dusty and dirty, the light of Christ will begin to filter through the darkness, touching and reviving your sagging spirit. It is this inner pilgrimage that is enhanced on retreat as you allow the Spirit of God to enter your sacred space – your inner life with all its secrets, dreams, emotional ups and downs, fears and wonderings. It is a place of deep longing for the healing love which God offers you, today, every day. In return, offer God as much of your self as you can; even if it seems a very small gift, it is precious to God.

Deepening

✠ Imagine yourself walking with Jesus – perhaps in a park or around your neighbourhood streets. Share with him whatever is on your mind.

Walking – making a pilgrimage

✠ If you have been on a pilgrimage somewhere already, spend some time reflecting on that experience and what has changed in your journey of faith since that time.

✠ Who are your 'travelling companions' on this retreat?

✠ Read an account of a modern pilgrimage, for example Joyce Rupp, *Walk in a Relaxed Manner: Life Lessons from the Camino*, Orbis, 2005: her account of walking the Santiago de Compostela pilgrim path in northern Spain.

Closing prayer

Jesus, my friend and brother,
my life pilgrimage is known to you;
its sidetracks and backtracks,
its doubt-full diversions,
the ways that have worried my soul.
But now I know, more surely
than I have ever known,
that you are my constant companion.
May I recognize you afresh each day,
share my self with you as fully as I can,
and be still enough to listen
as you share your Self with me.
AMEN

Or – a prayer from the past

Give me my scallop-shell[12] of quiet;
My staff of faith to walk upon;
My scrip of joy, immortal diet;
My bottle of salvation;
My gown of glory (hope's true gage);
And thus I'll take my pilgrimage.
(Sir Walter Raleigh, 1554–1618)

---

12 The scallop shell was worn as a sign of pilgrimage in the Middle Ages and may be found on pilgrim paths to this day.

On holiday with God

Being adventurous – *risk-taking*

Focus verse

Again, the kingdom of heaven is like a merchant in search of fine pearls; on finding one pearl of great value, he went and sold all that he had and bought it.
(Matthew 13.45–46)

Opening prayer

Lord,
some of us are risk-takers
and others of us are safety-first people.
In your love for us,
you invite us to extend our horizons,
you bring us greater freedom
to live with the risks that are
part of our growth in you.
Build our courage O God;
calm our nerves and
show us the beautiful danger
of being your children.
May we know that we are safe in you,
for all eternity.
AMEN

Scripture to use for lectio divina *or imaginative prayer*

¹⁰Now there was a disciple in Damascus named Ananias. The LORD said to him in a vision, 'Ananias.' He answered, 'Here I am, LORD.' ¹¹The LORD said to him, 'Get up and go to the street called Straight, and at the house of Judas look for a man of Tarsus named Saul. At this moment he is praying, ¹²and he has seen in a vision a man named Ananias come in and lay hands upon him so that he might regain his sight.' ¹³But Ananias answered, 'LORD, I have heard from many about this man, how much evil he has done to your saints in Jerusalem; ¹⁴and here he has authority from the chief priests to bind all who invoke your name.' ¹⁵But the LORD said to him, 'Go, for he is an instrument whom I have chosen to bring my name before Gentiles and kings and before the people of Israel; ¹⁶I myself will show him how much he must suffer for the sake of my name.' ¹⁷So Ananias went and entered the house. He laid his hands on Saul and said, 'Brother Saul, the LORD Jesus, who appeared to you on your way here, has sent me so that you may regain your sight and be filled with the Holy Spirit.' ¹⁸And immediately something like scales fell from his eyes, and his sight was restored. Then he got up and was baptized, ¹⁹and after taking some food, he regained his strength.
(Acts 9.10–19)

Personal reflection

🕯 Let your imagination connect you with the thoughts and feelings of Ananias as he hears the Lord's instructions and responds.

🕯 When have you been asked to do something that might put you at risk in some way? What was your response?

Further food for thought

When I think of risk-taking, I initially think of adventure tourism which gives willing daredevils the chance to be scared out of their wits at great cost! Here in New Zealand there are plenty of chances to get an adrenalin rush and, on a recent holiday, my husband and I came across some young people white-water rafting near Rotorua. We watched, fascinated, as, shrieking with anticipation, a group of young people in an inflatable raft dropped over the seven-metre Tutea waterfall, briefly disappeared into the froth and bubbles below and then popped to the surface like a cork, smiles of relief all over their faces! They were exhilarated by their adventure and so were we!!

But risk-taking with God is usually more subtle. It can *begin* with something as deceptively simple as plucking up the courage to make a phone call to an estranged relative, and then quietly escalate. It can mean contributing time and resources to an after-school programme full of children with profound social needs; it can mean leaving a well-paid job without knowing what lies ahead; it can mean travelling halfway around the world to do some aid work in an inhospitable environment, when you'd be far safer staying at home. Risk-taking with God can mean choosing to live entirely by faith, literally trusting God for what you need each day. Risk-taking with God can even mean putting your life on the line for what you believe in, as so many of our Christian forebears have done; even today, Christians in some countries take risks to fight injustice and are persecuted, even martyred for their faith.

Much of the risk-taking we do for God in the early stages of our journey of faith is hidden from view in the interior reaches of our mind and heart. Here, in our innermost being, the Holy Spirit initiates and enables the changes needed to put ourselves increasingly at God's disposal, for the service of God's people. Gradually we learn to let go of being swayed by what other people think or what might be sensible or prudent. And instead of trying to fool ourselves, we learn to face the fears and questions head on.

That was the case for Ananias as he wrestled with the task God was setting before him. He had made his 'here I am' response to God, and thought himself ready to listen, ready to serve. But what God asks of him scares him, and not without cause, for God was doing the equivalent of asking a child to walk into a lion's den. Ananias had heard of Saul's reputation for zealously seeking out, arresting and imprisoning followers of Christ in Jerusalem; he no doubt knew that Saul had watched the stoning of Steven and had 'approved of their killing him' (Acts 8.1). Now Saul was there in Damascus with 'authority from the chief priests' (Acts 9.14), and instead of warning Ananias to keep away from this persecutor of the church, God is telling him to go to Saul and lay hands upon his eyes so his sight could be restored.

Ananias doesn't go at once. But he is not procrastinating or grumbling to himself. Instead, he puts his very natural fears directly to God and waits for God's clarifying reply. Ananias is then given the privilege of hearing God's vision for Saul – the *wonder and responsibility* of spreading the good news across the known world, and the *cost* of that vocation – to 'suffer for the sake of God's name' (Acts 9.16). Saul would, in the process of spreading the gospel, experience for himself the sort of persecution and violence that he had witnessed or inflicted on others. Just as Peter was freed from the shackles of his shameful betrayal of Jesus to become the rock on which the new church would be built, so Saul would have a new beginning and, through his zeal and his suffering, a chance to make a difference for God, building up God's people instead of hunting them down. Seeing with refreshed vision, Saul would take a new name – Paul – illustrating his intention to act with humility, to see himself as of little account in the eyes of the world, as he risked everything to do the will and work of God.

Ananias knows in his spirit that this task from God is part of God's greater purpose. His inner reluctance is transformed into willing obedience, so he agrees to go to Saul in spite of Saul's reputation. What grace there is in Ananias' attitude and in his words to Saul:

> Brother Saul, the LORD Jesus, who appeared to you
> on your way here, has sent me so that you may
> regain your sight and be filled with the Holy Spirit.
> (Acts 9.17)

The confused, isolated blind man, wondering perhaps if he was going out of his mind, is touched by the kind hands of the stranger whom God had said would come to him. Importantly, Paul's experience of Jesus on the Damascus Road is authenticated by Ananias, and then he experiences three gifts – the regaining of his sight, the infilling of the Spirit of God and the sacrament of baptism. These powerful, healing, equipping gifts are strong and unequivocal; they needed to be, so the memory of that day would never leave Paul and, in his darkest moments, in prison or in pain, he would be able to recall his conversion, the amazing symmetry of his prayer and Ananias' arrival, and God's purpose for his life.

This new beginning became possible because Ananias was willing to take a risk for the God he knew, worshipped and obeyed. As he stepped out, trusting God would provide whatever he needed to fulfil this significant task, Ananias changed too. He grew through this experience – his trust in God deepened and so did his own sense of joy in being part of the working-out of God's vision. Through the Holy Spirit, he found the courage he needed to venture into 'the lion's den' and, perhaps surprisingly, discovered within himself a real compassion for the vulnerable man, this 'brother Saul' whom he had considered an 'enemy'. The words Ananias needed were on his lips without planning or effort, as the Spirit of God touched and blessed both men.

When we take a holiday with God we risk discovering things about ourselves that we didn't know before. But we do this in the knowledge that God wants the best for us and will not force growth, or insight, or even love upon us, if we are tentative in opening to the workings of the Spirit. The pace of growth is determined by our willingness to take the risk of being honest before God: *facing* our own inadequacies and foibles so we can draw on God's healing, and *acknowledging* our abilities and experience so they can be used for God.

As we grow in the likeness of Christ, as we are strengthened in our inner being (Ephesians 3.16), we are more able to take individual and group action to right wrongs, to protest against injustice or environmental damage, to make our voices heard against ongoing systemic abuses of power by governments and corporate giants. One voice may seem like a weak flame in the face of a water cannon wielded by 'powers and principalities' but, gathered together, the small flames can strengthen and spread. What starts off as a simple act of courage and conviction by individuals, can become something much greater: a catalyst for a wider movement which, over time, can have implications for a whole nation or even the whole world. I think of the Maori prophets Te Whiti and Tohu at Parihaka in New Zealand who, drawing on their own traditions, on the Bible and Jesus' injunction to love your enemies, inspired a determined and creative passive resistance movement which disrupted the advance of settlers hungry for land. Te Whiti and Tohu would not have considered themselves to be charismatic leaders or outstanding political tacticians, but they were prepared to risk imprisonment and exile, rather than sit back and let injustices associated with the after-effects of the New Zealand Land Wars continue.

In the twentieth century, risks were taken by many to ensure the fall of the Berlin Wall and the dismantling of Apartheid in South Africa. More recently in the Middle East, individuals are taking risks to rise up against totalitarian regimes.

Maybe God is inviting *you* to take action for the sake of those you care about, and do your part, however small, in the healing of the world. This task may be something out of the public eye, something that you and God know requires trust and courage and greater dependency on the guidance of the Holy Spirit. Even if God gives you an opportunity or task that initially scares you, remember what Ananias did – he expressed his honest feelings and fears to God directly – and what God did – he provided for Ananias courage, compassion, and the right words for the one who had been an enemy.

Little by little we can learn to live God's instruction, 'to act justly and to love mercy and to walk humbly' with our God (Micah 6:8b), even if, like the merchant who sold all he had to buy the pearl of great price, this means taking a risk, ignoring conventional wisdom, setting aside the approval of others and our own personal comfort, so that the kingdom of heaven may increase.

Being adventurous – risk-taking

Deepening

✠ Spend some time with God reflecting on your own 'risk-taking' profile; share with God your longing to be free to respond to God's invitations to grow in faith.

✠ Think about the context of your own life: where you live, who is advantaged and disadvantaged, and ask God to help you discern how you might begin to be involved in making a difference.

✠ Pray with this portion of Paul's letter to the Ephesians, and as you do so, remember the journey that Paul had made to reach this point of deep understanding of the love of God:

> [16]I pray that out of his glorious riches he may strengthen you with power through his Spirit in your inner being, [17]so that Christ may dwell in your hearts through faith. And I pray that you, being rooted and established in love, [18]may have power, together with all the LORD's holy people, to grasp how wide and long and high and deep is the love of Christ, [19]and to know this love that surpasses knowledge – that you may be filled to the measure of all the fullness of God.
> (Ephesians 3.16–19)

✠ Who has made a difference in your life, for the better?
Give thanks to God for these people, living or departed.

Closing prayer

Loving God,
you who inspire unlikely champions
to do your work for justice and peace,
inspire me that I may become more like Jesus,
that I may grow in courage, wisdom and vision,
and make a difference to your beautiful world.
AMEN

On holiday with God

Anywhere – *meeting the marginalized*

Focus verse

The spirit of the LORD GOD is upon me,
because the LORD has anointed me;
he has sent me to bring good news to the oppressed,
to bind up the broken-hearted,
to proclaim liberty to the captives,
and release to the prisoners ...
(Isaiah 61.1)

Opening prayer

Jesus, you accept people.
That is your gift and grace.
But to be honest,
I struggle with those who are
different, who inhabit
the edges of our society.
The unpredictable,
the dirty or deranged,
the ones who beg or bleat
unleash not my best self,
but the one within who turns away
and does not want to know.
I am ashamed of that part of me
but it's there and you know it.
And you want to redeem it,
if I will let you.
Please.
Yes.
Do.
AMEN

Scripture to use for lectio divina *or imaginative prayer*

¹¹On the way to Jerusalem Jesus was going through the region between Samaria and Galilee. ¹²As he entered a village, ten lepers approached him. Keeping their distance, ¹³they called out, saying, 'Jesus, Master, have mercy on us!' ¹⁴When he saw them, he said to them, 'Go and show yourselves to the priests.' And as they went, they were made clean. ¹⁵Then one of them, when he saw that he was healed, turned back, praising God with a loud voice. ¹⁶He prostrated himself at Jesus' feet and thanked him. And he was a Samaritan. ¹⁷Then Jesus asked, 'Were not ten made clean? But the other nine, where are they? ¹⁸Was none of them found to return and give praise to God except this foreigner?' ¹⁹Then he said to him, 'Get up and go on your way; your faith has made you well.' (Luke 17.11–19)

Personal reflection

߈ From this familiar story, what has touched your heart or your mind?

߈ Who might the 'lepers' be in your context?

Further food for thought

I would rather not explore this difficult topic but it requires inclusion, first because we encounter people who are 'different' wherever we go, on holiday or in our local High Street; second, because Jesus spent so much of his earthly ministry among the suffering, the disempowered, the outcasts and the poor; and third because there are parts of ourselves we are reluctant to acknowledge (our own 'lepers'), the parts that are greedy, selfish, proud and lazy.

This Scripture passage is just one of many which illustrate the plight of the 'lepers' – their sense of exclusion from normal community living, their fear of others' responses, their desperation for something that would change their sorry circumstances – and the truth of human forgetfulness even when God has met us and changed us forever. We are reminded that gratitude does not come easily for most of us.

Whether marked by a physical disability, mental illness, poverty or social disapproval, those on the margins were constantly the focus of Jesus' ministry of mercy and healing. It follows then, that if we want to become more like Jesus, at some point we will be confronted by our attitudes to those who are 'different' or far from 'perfect'. We will have to consider how we are going to respond to the needs of the 'widows and orphans' and other disadvantaged people in our neighbourhood and beyond. And we will be challenged to allow God to help us integrate those less attractive parts of our personality so we can stop projecting these aspects of ourselves onto other people.

I have a vivid memory of visiting Moscow in 2004. On the pavement outside the railings around the recently rebuilt Cathedral of Christ the Saviour in all its magnificence, sat an older woman, shapeless beneath shabby clothes and a torn shawl. I do not recall her face, but she had a bowl beside her and held it up as we left our tourist bus, clearly hoping that we would give her something, anything. Did I drop a few roubles into her bowl? To this day I am ashamed to say, 'No'. Why? Because I was not 'present' to her reality and I shut up my compassion (1 John 3.17). Instead I was so preoccupied by my intention to buy a genuine, hand-painted Russian icon, that I simply passed her by. But the story does not end there.

I went into that most beautiful cathedral shimmering with natural light, white marble, glorious gilding, freshly painted frescoes, walls of apostles and saints with their rich golden haloes, and the high and holy images of Jesus as Pantocrator[13], as Saviour, as infant held in Mary's arms. It was impressive, awe-inspiring and an amazing testament to the determination of the Russian people to rebuild their sacred centre, after the original Cathedral was dynamited on Stalin's instructions in the 1930s.

In the few minutes left before our tour was due to depart, I went into the shop where dozens of Russian women were looking for mementos to take home. I looked for the icon that would speak

---

13 'Pantocrator' (Greek). Usually referred to as 'Almighty' or 'Christ in Majesty', this particular iconographic depiction is common in Orthodox Christianity.

to my soul so I could purchase it as I had hoped, but the most appealing, on the shelves behind the counter, were priced well beyond my budget. I glanced down and, resting quietly on the bottom of the display box that formed the counter, lay a smaller icon of Christ, clear and pure. Jesus' wise, sad eyes, given penetrating power through the icon, met mine. Thoughts of buying an icon dissolved under his gaze: I knew that he knew my failure to love my neighbour. His face that day touches me still.

I'd like to be able to say that I was changed forever at that point and found generosity continuously welling up inside me – but that wouldn't be true. Although I am getting braver, being around those who are profoundly disabled, those who are mentally unwell or somehow 'different' is still challenging for me. Perhaps it is for you too, because we are naturally more comfortable with people who are like us. But Jesus confronts us with our complacency, asking us to look at our selfishness and the thinking patterns that inhibit our compassion. He invites us to do what he did, 'eating with sinners and tax collectors' (Mark 2.16) or their modern equivalents.

Fear and selfishness are the fundamental but often unacknowledged barriers behind our reluctance to engage with people who are unwell, unfed, unloved. We fear their 'distressing disguise', as Mother Teresa would say. We fear that 'they' might make a call on our lives, ease their way into our comfortable existences and upset our routines: 'Give them an inch and they'll take a mile'. I remember hearing a speaker at a conference years ago who invited us to imagine Jesus being a welcome guest in our home – for the first week or two – until he starts asking the equivalent of local lepers into the house. Jesus' direct application of gospel living is too much of a threat to our personal comfort, the speaker said, and so we look for a solution: lock Jesus in a cupboard under the stairs and place a table with flowers and a candle outside! Far safer and easier to control!

And that is the other underlying factor – keeping control. None of us likes to be thought of as a 'control freak', but the reality is that many of us want things done 'our way', make no room for other opinions, have to have the last word, and are sure that we know what is best for those around us.

We even want to control how much of ourselves we give to God, afraid that if we give God an inch, God will take a mile or will want us to give up something or someone we cherish. So we welcome Jesus into the 'nice' parts of our lives, do good works and say the right things, but when it comes to actually giving more of ourselves to the more of God, we resist. Instead of longing to get closer to a God who is on our side, keen to help us grow in fulfilment of our potential, wanting to guide and sustain us in our life's work, we hold God at arms' length, in case God gets too close, in case God asks too much.

Who is the God we are resisting? The Jesus who looked at me through that icon over seven years ago was not a punitive, accusing God but a God who compassionately helped me see deeper into my soul so I could face the truth of some of the shadow that lies there on the margins of my mind, waiting to be accepted.

This God invites you, invites me to 'sit down and eat' with the parts of ourselves that we'd rather disown. God knows that, as we become kinder to ourselves, as we acknowledge our own potential for violence or pettiness, our capacity for compassion expands. And then we can respond when God invites us to 'sit down and eat' with those people whom we want to avoid. We can let those on the margins become real to us, people with names and stories and pains and hopes.

Once we own our inner brokenness and ugliness, we can look with compassion on others' brokenness or ugliness and see the image of Christ within that person. The differences of which we were so afraid evaporate in the face of our common humanity and vulnerability. That sense of deep connectedness to the whole of God's world will be enriched and expanded as our embrace widens to include both the 'leper within' and the 'lepers' of our time: the gang member, the drug addict, the dispossessed and poor, the unwanted elderly, the teenage mum ... the list is unending.

I carry with me the memory of that old Russian woman – it may be that one day I will meet her in heaven. If so, I will face her and give her my apology. I will listen to her story and, through the mercy of Jesus, be blessed by her forgiveness.

Deepening

✠ If there have been times when you have failed to act with compassion and love, pray with this passage and let God meet you in your regret and offer you forgiveness:

'How does God's love abide in anyone who has the world's goods and sees a brother or sister in need and yet refuses help? (1 John 3.17)

✠ What part/s of yourself do you try to ignore or hide from others? Invite the Spirit of Jesus into those 'leper' parts of yourself – allow yourself to be open to healing and integration as you journey towards wholeness.

✠ What part does gratitude play in your life?

✠ What is your experience of living or working with someone whom others revile or avoid? How does your faith affect your capacity to be present to that person?

Closing prayer

Compassionate and all-knowing God,
thank you for your faithful love and concern.
Thank you for your grace towards me
in spite of my weakness and wilfulness.
Help me to learn from my mistakes.
Help me to be open to sharing more of
what you have given to me with others,
with those who live different lives,
who struggle to make ends meet,
who need to be held and cherished
instead of harassed or criticized.
May your love flow through me
in word and touch and deed
to your glory, not mine.
AMEN

On holiday with God

Facing the unexpected – *suffering*

Focus verse

He was despised and rejected by others; a man of sorrows, and acquainted with grief ... (Isaiah 53.3a)

Opening prayer

Sometimes, O God,
my life takes a tumble
and I fall headlong
into hopelessness and pain.
Sometimes I wonder
how much I can take
of suffering, of searing sorrow;
I grope my way through
the fog of each day,
hoping that when I reach out,
someone will be there
to hold my hand.
In the night-time of my distress
you are that Hand-holder.
In the day-time of my dreary desperation
you are that Someone.
You, O God in Christ,
know my human life,
intimately,
painfully,
to the point of death.
But that is not the end of it.
You, O God in Christ,
bring me, bring us all,
to new life in you,
with you, for you,
forever.
AMEN

Facing the unexpected – suffering

Scripture to use for lectio divina or imaginative prayer

[36]Then Jesus went with them to a place called Gethsemane; and he said to his disciples, 'Sit here while I go over there and pray.' [37]He took with him Peter and the two sons of Zebedee, and began to be grieved and agitated. [38]Then he said to them, 'I am deeply grieved, even to death; remain here and stay awake with me.'

[39]And going a little farther, he threw himself on the ground and prayed, 'My Father, if it is possible, let this cup pass from me; yet not what I want but what you want.' [40]Then he came to his disciples and found them sleeping; and he said to Peter, 'So, could you not stay awake with me one hour?'
(Matthew 26.36–40)

Personal reflection

§ Allow yourself the time to enter this pivotal part of the Christian faith story as fully as your imagination and sensitivity will allow. What emerges from this experience for you?

§ In your understanding, how does the suffering of Jesus relate to the suffering of human beings?

Further food for thought

We often struggle to acknowledge our own suffering, avoiding it by pressing on with schedules and responsibilities, or denying it by delaying seeking support or advice. Instead of taking the time to face our suffering and make it part of our prayer, we can minimize or downplay its effect on us by comparing our experience with others. Their situation is so much worse, we think, and so we push the pain down deep inside our soul. Perhaps you've been down that track yourself. Perhaps you've put your own pain – physical or mental – to one side, because you've felt that you shouldn't 'make a fuss' or 'bother people', yet inside you are longing for someone to hear, really hear the truth of your situation. Perhaps you have always found it difficult to ask for what you need, to claim the time or love or resources for your wellbeing, and when suffering comes your way, it has been hard to admit your need to others.

There are always people with greater loads to carry than we have, that's true, but the reality is that however 'great' or 'small' our suffering is in our own eyes, our God wants to be there with us in the midst of it, to bring comfort and hope. God wants to meet *you* in *your* need if you will 'open the door' to your innermost feelings, fears and thoughts and share them with God in prayer.

The silence and the stillness of retreat time allows that door to begin to open, so don't be surprised if something from your unexamined past or busy present life turns up on the doorstep of your mind. That something could be to do with an old grief, an unhealed emotional wound, a deep longing, or whatever God illuminates as a first step towards its healing.

When that something emerges, unwelcome though it may initially be, you have a choice. You can continue to pretend that everything is fine when you know it is not, and risk spiritual and psychological stagnation, or you can recognize that this is a movement of God for your good, and co-operate with the Holy Spirit who will soothe and console you, and gently challenge and equip you for the way ahead.

One of the things people often say when painful material comes to the surface again is, 'I thought I had dealt with that!' Perhaps that's what you might think too. Often people *have* dealt with something as best they could at an earlier point. But as our circumstances change, as we get stronger in our faith, God is able to offer us more healing, invites us to greater self-understanding and calls forth from us more courage, so we can enter the suffering and darkness which may be holding us back from the fullness of life that God offers.

What do you do when a partially examined grief turns up on retreat, a memory of abuse breaks through to consciousness, or a guilty act cries out for confession? First, you can trust God's intention: that this has happened because of God's desire to bring you to healing. Second, you can trust the timing: on retreat you have an opportunity to address something fundamental to your wellbeing while you have the time to devote to reflection, prayer, weeping, writing or anger, as you move towards the glimmer of resurrection dawn. Third, you can trust the promise of Scripture that when you confess your sins, God is faithful and will forgive you and cleanse you from any kind of wrong (1 John 1.9). And finally, you can trust the provision of God: you can be assured that, as you turn to the Holy Spirit for guidance, a way forward will be found, at a pace that you can handle and in a way that does not frighten or overwhelm you.

Our own suffering is difficult enough to face, but when we are exposed to the suffering of others, we are confronted by our own powerlessness, the fact that we cannot 'fix' this or make it go away. We are confronted too by our culturally driven expectation of a quick solution, and perhaps most awkwardly, we are confronted by the implications of the way we imagine God works in the world – our image of God. And so it happens that, as we sit with people in pain, as we see our world's struggles splashed casually across our screens to the point of desensitization, as we recognize that suffering can enter our lives at any moment, we may well ask that most uncomfortable question: 'What is the nature of a God who seems powerless to stop suffering in its many forms?'

⛬ Over the centuries, thousands of words have been written in response to this question and, if you prefer, you can stop reading right now and give some time to your own wonderings and response before reading on.

God does not inflict suffering on us; suffering happens through the application of natural laws which govern the way the world works (gravity, for example), through others' mistakes or sin, through our own genetic make-up or life choices, through the exercise of free will and through the natural expressions of a creation which is still 'groaning' as if in labour (Romans 8.22).

In the Old Testament, the consistent theme is of a God who seeks deep, committed, covenant relationship with creation, with all of humanity. With the birth of Jesus, God's nature as Love is given sharper focus. The writings of the Gospels (for example John 3.16 and 15.1–11), Acts and the Epistles (for example

Romans 8.38–39; Ephesians 3.14–19; 1 John 4.7) and the ongoing mission of the church, however imperfect that might be, proclaim that Love again and again and again. We can begin to glimpse the way a loving God works in our world as we love our own children and help them grow to adulthood and responsible decision-making. Such a love, as we know from experience, cannot stop bad things happening, but it can be there for the long haul as the consequences unfold and the long road to healing or reconciliation is travelled.

As chaplain at an aged care village, I see families faced with the unpredictability of the dying process. Like natural birth, dying runs its own course and will not be hurried for the sake of our sensibilities. A need to know when our ailing loved one will die is often born of a desire for their suffering to end, but also, whether we recognize it or not, a desire for our own powerlessness and frustration to cease. Even with good pain management and symptom control, it is hard to watch someone's life on this earth come to an end; it is hard to sit beside a loved mum or dad and count the seconds between breaths as the body winds down; it is hard to simply 'be' when we are so accustomed to taking action and there seems to be 'nothing to do' but wait.

But 'being' and 'waiting' is precisely what we are called to 'do' when we are with those who are suffering, the sick, the dying, the bereaved. We don't have to have wise words of comfort, we just need to turn up and spend time with those whom society may set to one side, hide or even discard. By our being with them, we re-present the compassion of Christ and connect them with that great Love which suffers *with* them, and *with* us.

Perhaps you can remember being ill as a child and having a parent or loved care-giver sit with you as you drifted between waking and sleeping? Security and comfort and hope came, not necessarily through conversation, but through the *presence* of the one who loved you, who would gladly have changed places with you, who held your hand or sang to you or simply sat and kept you company.

That's what Jesus longed for in Gethsemane when he asked his disciples to watch with him for a little while. He needed their presence, their solidarity, their loving concern expressed by their companionship. And they let him down. They couldn't stand to see his clear and abject suffering, so they absented themselves from his inner anguish by taking refuge in sleep.

Jesus' personal struggle in Gethsemane is, at a purely human level, like the suffering of any of us who face a painful or untimely death. Even though his relationship with his Father is deep and true and reliable, he, as we all must some day, finds himself alone as he considers his impending death. Jesus has to find a way through and, for him, that way is to re-dedicate himself to the greater purposes of God, and accept the way of the cross. Not only does he experience humiliation and extreme physical pain, Jesus endures mental and spiritual anguish beyond all imagining, culminating in a terrible sense of separation from God as Jesus takes upon himself the sinfulness of the world. Sin's power is put to death with him on the cross. Jesus rises to new life, but the power of sin over humanity is defeated for all time.

Because of what Jesus was prepared to suffer as a human being and as God; through Jesus' presence in human history alongside us, we are able to say that we have a God who *knows* suffering, not theoretically but intimately, through the lived experience of the second person of the Trinity. And that knowing makes all the difference – we indeed have a God who *is with us*, Emmanuel, flesh of our flesh and spirit of God's Spirit, knowing what it's like to gasp for breath, and feel the pain of wounding.

We all have things which bring us to our knees, overwhelmed by our own suffering or the suffering of others. What we do when we are in that place of vulnerability will depend on how we see God. If we trust that Jesus is there with us in solidarity, we can tell him how we feel, we can reach out and, in our imagination, grasp his hand. As we do so, our suffering can be transformed, even transcended, by the grace of God. We will experience the mysterious reality of that 'peace of God which surpasses all understanding' (Philippians 4.7) and, as this prayer found at the Ravensbrück Concentration Camp so movingly suggests, we can have faith that no suffering is wasted in the economy of God:

LORD
Remember not only the men and women of good will
but all those of ill will.

Do not only remember all the sufferings they have subjected us
to.

Remember the fruits we brought forth thanks to this suffering –
Our comradeship,
Our loyalty,
Our humility,
Our courage and generosity,
the greatness of heart that all of this inspired.

And when they come to judgement,
let all those fruits we have borne
be their reward
and their forgiveness. AMEN

The love of God is forged in the fire of suffering. This love is infinite, eternal and all-embracing; it is also intimate, cherishing and personal.

God loves *you* – take hold of that truth and begin to live it, today.

Deepening

✠ Consider the Ravensbrück Prayer. What does it say to you about the nature of suffering and of God?

✠ Reflect on the passage below and then rewrite the italicized part to include your own challenges:

Who will separate us from the love of Christ? *Will hardship, or distress, or persecution, or famine, or nakedness, or sword, or peril?* No, in all these things we are more than conquerors through him who loved us.
(Romans 8.35, 37)

✠ Reflect on your own history of suffering and any questions or struggles which you experienced. Don't hesitate to bring the strong feelings or confusion to God.

Closing prayer

Jesus,
I am in awe of you ...
and the way you absorbed the suffering of the world
and bear it still today.
Thank you that I can bring my truth to you
when I face suffering,
or weep for the suffering of others;
you want to take my pain, all our pain,
and hold it in your heart
until it is transformed by grace
and begins to be shaped into
action and gratitude,
into hope and hallelujahs.
AMEN

On holiday with God

Eating together – *growing in intimacy*

Focus verse

'Listen! I am standing at the door, knocking; if you hear my voice
and open the door, I will come in to you and eat with you, and
you with me.'
(Revelation 3.20)

Opening prayer

Jesus,
an old hymn tells me that you are
lover of my soul.
Lover.
I wriggle under the implication of
that word.
For if you are lover of my soul,
you long for a response
to show you
that I have seen you for who you truly are
– gentlest Love
– warming my heart
– stirring my desire
    for more of you ...
        and more of you ...
           and more of you ...
until I am lost in the mystery
of being with you,
in you, of you,
totally,
utterly,
One.
Help me to risk drawing closer to you today.
AMEN

Scripture to use for lectio divina *or imaginative prayer*

³⁶A Pharisee invited Jesus to have dinner with him, and Jesus went to his house and sat down to eat. ³⁷In that town was a woman who lived a sinful life. She heard that Jesus was eating in the Pharisee's house, so she brought an alabaster jar full of perfume ³⁸and stood behind Jesus, by his feet, crying and wetting his feet with her tears. Then she dried his feet with her hair, kissed them, and poured the perfume on them. ³⁹When the Pharisee saw this, he said to himself, 'If this man really were a prophet, he would know who this woman is who is touching him; he would know what kind of sinful life she lives!' ⁴⁰Jesus spoke up and said to him, 'Simon, I have something to tell you.' 'Yes, Teacher,' he said, 'tell me.' ⁴¹'There were two men who owed money to a moneylender,' Jesus began. 'One owed him five hundred silver coins, and the other one fifty. ⁴²Neither of them could pay him back, so he cancelled the debts of both. Which one, then, will love him more?' ⁴³'I suppose', answered Simon, 'that it would be the one who was forgiven more.' 'You are right', said Jesus. ⁴⁴Then he turned to the woman and said to Simon, 'Do you see this woman? I came into your home, and you gave me no water for my feet, but she has washed my feet with her tears and dried them with her hair. ⁴⁵You did not welcome me with a kiss, but she has not stopped kissing my feet since I came. ⁴⁶You provided no olive oil for my head, but she has covered my feet with perfume. ⁴⁷I tell you, then, the great love she has shown proves that her many sins have been forgiven. But whoever has been forgiven little shows only a little love.' ⁴⁸Then Jesus said to the woman, 'Your sins are forgiven.' ⁴⁹The others sitting at the table began to say to themselves, 'Who is this, who even forgives sins?' ⁵⁰But Jesus said to the woman, 'Your faith has saved you; go in peace.'
(Luke 7.36–50 Good News Bible)

Personal reflection

§ What do you make of this powerful story as you engage with it in your imagination?

§ What strikes you as significant about the relationships between Simon and Jesus, and between the woman and Jesus?

Further food for thought

Stories of hospitality flow through the scriptures like a warm toffee treat. In Genesis 18.1–8, for example, when Abraham entertains the Holy One in the guise of three angels, we see the customary offering and receiving of hospitality in a context of respect and tradition. In Luke 1, Jesus' earthly story begins with the obedience of Mary whose hospitable womb enables Emmanuel, God with us, to take physical flesh. In Luke 22, as Jesus inaugurates the Eucharistic feast, we see something of the tension and poignancy of his last meal with those closest to him. The simple meal in the Passover tradition takes on new life and meaning as Jesus himself becomes the sacrificial lamb.

God longs for you to 'taste and *see* that the LORD is good' (Psalm 34.8), to eat and drink of the riches of God's love for you as you rest and reflect on your retreat. God wants to nourish you, not with the dregs or the leftovers but with the best, the sweetest: 'I would feed you with the finest of the wheat, and with honey from the rock I would satisfy you' (Psalm 81.16).

But the sad reality is that many of us are starving, turning down God's invitation to dinner, denying ourselves the goodness and fullness of God, and looking elsewhere for fulfilment. It is only when we realize that nothing but God will satisfy us that we begin a *metanoia*, a turning back towards the waiting arms of our God, and take up the journey towards the *intimacy* that God offers.

Last year, when I watched the block-busting science fiction film *Avatar*, I was struck by the greeting and response given between the Na'vi, the humanoid native inhabitants of a moon named Pandora. The freshness of '*I see you*' touched me deeply and expressed a quality of intimacy that is rarely shown in our perfunctory greeting rituals of 'Hello', 'Hi!' or 'How are you?', answered with the socially expected, rarely honest, 'Fine, thanks'.

God sees you with all your uncertainties and hopefulness, your anxiety and your dreams, and wants to bring you to a place where you realize that you don't have to pretend any more, you don't have to do anything to make God love you. You are invited to snuggle up close to the heart of God and rest from all that tires or tries you. This is an invitation to intimacy, to enjoy God's love and unconditional understanding and acceptance which your soul craves:

As a deer longs for flowing streams,
so my soul longs for you, O God.
My soul thirsts for God,
for the living God.
(Psalm 42.1–2a)

Intimacy is at the centre of our earlier passage of Scripture in which Jesus is invited to dine with Simon the Pharisee, an upstanding member of the local community. The other main character in this story is an unnamed woman of doubtful reputation, who has heard and taken to heart the good news of forgiveness and healing that Jesus has been proclaiming. As a result, she wants to offer thanksgiving for her restored sense of self-worth and dignity, and the hope of a different future, so she finds out where Jesus is and takes her oil as an offering, aware that she is entering a setting where she may face ridicule, or worse.

With those Jesus loved and who loved him, people like the siblings Mary, Martha and Lazarus in Bethany, or Peter's family at Capernaum, a dinner invitation would not simply be about a meal. It would be about rest and relaxation, conversations unfolding and 'heart-to-heart' connection. But this personal, restorative dimension was absent from Simon's invitation because Jesus had been invited to Simon's house so he could be cross-examined by the Pharisees. To show his disdain, Simon does not accord Jesus any of the accepted gestures of welcome – no water to wash dusty feet, no kiss of greeting, no oil for anointing of head or beard.

Instead the respect Jesus should be given is denied and he is placed in the awkward position of being an invited – but dishonoured – guest, before the meal even begins.

The woman is no fool – she sees this disrespectful and deliberate withholding of normal hospitality, and she begins to weep. She knows what it is like to be treated as a person of little worth, or to walk into a trap set by those who think they have more power. She had come hoping to make a quiet gesture of gratitude, but in her empathy for Jesus, she makes herself vulnerable to further slurs on her character by breaking open her ointment jar, anointing Jesus' feet and wiping them with her hair. In the eyes of all but Jesus this was a shocking thing to do, for a Jewish woman kept her hair covered, and let it down only at home for her husband. This *physically* intimate outpouring of compassion stuns the gathered religious leaders, but they are unlikely to recognize the deeper intimacy of *heart* and *mind*: the woman *sees* Jesus for who he really is, and he *sees* her passionate gift of care and knows it flows from a place of deep gratitude and love.

Jesus affirms her actions but, in no uncertain terms, he tells Simon what he thinks of his lack of hospitality, using a very simple story to try to get the message of radical grace through to Simon. Simon is hesitant in his response to Jesus' question, but the woman recognizes herself in the story right away as the one who owed the greater debt. What joy for her to hear Jesus describing, in the parable, the dynamics which had led to her being there with him, his feet wet with her tears, fragrant with her perfume. She had great need of grace and, knowing herself to be forgiven, her 'debt cancelled', had responded with this great act of love for which she will be remembered as long as the stories of Scripture are shared.

Some translations of this passage imply that she was forgiven *because* she had come to Jesus and wept and anointed and shown remorse, but Jesus makes it clear that the woman's actions had not been done *in order to earn forgiveness*. He speaks to her to confirm what she already knew – she had been forgiven much, and was therefore giving much in return. That is the natural movement of grace – we receive the grace of God and *in gratitude* we reach out to others: we are forgiven and so we are more able to forgive; we are consoled and, seeing others' situations with more empathy, we can offer consolation (2 Corinthians 1.3–4).

The spiritual journey is a series of movements towards intimacy with God. Over time, through the work of the Holy Spirit, the protective layers of habit, duty, role and responsibility begin to dissolve until our souls stand before God, no longer supported or hidden by all the things we have used to bolster or defend our sense of self over the course of a lifetime.

You may already know the truth of this journey – the struggles to 'practise what you preach'; the battle of the will as you seek to do something beautiful for God but are sabotaged by the desire to ensure your own comfort; the repeated failures to live up to your own expectations; the letting go of cherished ways of seeing yourself as you accept the shadow parts of your personality; the little moments of mystery when you encounter a touch of the divine and are moved to your very essence; the glimpse of a prayer answered, a problem solved or an unexpected way forward opening up before you; the indescribable joy when you know you are in the right place at the right time and God has used your presence and personhood to touch another human heart. For a moment you and God are united in ministry, heart to heart and mind to mind in divine intimacy.

We are both light and shadow, made of strong stuff but also of cloud and feathers, flighty and changeable. If we are willing, the spiritual journey will challenge our beliefs, taking us from places of unexamined certainty about the nature of God, into the maelstrom of searching and questioning as we deconstruct earlier concepts of faith. If we persevere, we will emerge into a 'broad space' in which the 'both/and' of life, its paradoxes and complexities, are held lightly by hands that know their own sinfulness *and* their own holiness. If we are willing, the spiritual journey will take us from familiar patterns of verbal prayer, to moments of stillness, to a stance of receptivity rather than activity. We may find that old prayer patterns no longer satisfy our yearnings and we are drawn to the simplicity of 'being' with God, opening our hearts more and more to the deep work of the Spirit within, as we settle into the silence of contemplation, where we allow ourselves to be loved to our core.

Eating together – growing in intimacy

In this process, the God whom Jesus addressed as 'Abba', an intimate term akin to 'daddy' (see Mark 14.36), is given more and more room in our lives until the Spirit of God indwells us as fully as is possible in this earthly life, and we know ourselves to be beloved, safe, accepted and truly seen. From this place of deep intimacy and security we are empowered to offer the profound hospitality of God to those we meet day by day.

Deepening

✠ Reflect on an experience of hospitality which enabled you to feel loved and accepted.

✠ Pray with Luke 22.14–27 – the Lord's supper.

✠ When have you felt in great need of God's grace?
When have you felt as if a 'great debt' has been cancelled?

✠ What changes have you experienced in your prayer life?
What do you think about the movement from vocal prayer to the prayer of quiet, contemplative prayer? Talk to God about your prayer practice and hopes ... and then spend some time listening. ☺

Closing prayer

For meditation: a fifteenth-century hymn by Bianco de Siena[14]

Come down, O Love divine,
Seek thou this soul of mine,
And visit it with thine own ardour glowing;
O Comforter draw near,
Within my heart appear,
And kindle it, thy holy flame bestowing ...

O let it freely burn,
Till earthly passions turn
To dust and ashes in its heat consuming;
And let thy glorious light,
Shine ever on my sight,
And clothe me round, the while my path illuming.

Let holy charity
Mine outward vesture be,
And lowliness become mine inner clothing:
True lowliness of heart,
Which takes the humbler part,
And o'er its own shortcomings weeps with loathing.

And so the yearning strong,
With which the soul will long
Shall far outpass the power of human telling;
For none can guess its grace,
Till he become the place
Wherein the Holy Spirit makes his dwelling.

---

14 Translated by R. F. Littledale, Number 235, *Hymns Ancient and Modern Revised*, Canterbury Press.

On holiday with God

By the pool – *opening to healing*

Focus verse

'Do you want to be made well?'
(John 5.6b)

Opening prayer

God of all power,
God of all love,
healing and holiness flow from you
in currents of compassion.
Help me to float in that
sacred stream
so your grace can touch me,
cleanse me
and move me
wherever you will.
AMEN

Scripture to use for lectio divina *or imaginative prayer*

²Now in Jerusalem by the Sheep Gate there is a pool, called in Hebrew Bethesda, which has five porticoes. ³In these lay many invalids – blind, lame and paralysed. ⁵One man was there who had been ill for thirty-eight years. ⁶When Jesus saw him lying there and knew that he had been there a long time, he said to him, 'Do you want to be made well?' ⁷The sick man answered, 'Sir, I have no one to put me into the pool when the water is stirred up; and while I am making my way, someone else steps down ahead of me.' ⁸Jesus said to him, 'Stand up, take your mat and walk.' ⁹At once the man was made well and he took up his mat and began to walk.
(John 5.1–9)

By the pool – opening to healing

Personal reflection

§ What are you noticing as you pray with this Scripture with heart and mind open to God's leading?

§ What questions are raised for you as you think about healing in the context of your faith and life experience?

Further food for thought

Nowadays 'health tourism' is gathering momentum as people try to access care or cure not readily or reasonably available in their own country. It is not a new phenomenon; people travelled in search of healing in the Middle Ages, visiting holy sites such as Canterbury or Holywell, where you can still see crutches left behind more recently by those whose lives were changed forever. To this day people visit places like Walsingham in Norfolk or Lourdes in France, seeking the healing that tradition assures them is possible for those who make the journey in faith.

Does God *still* heal?

For some readers, there may be acute pain around the whole question of healing: you may have watched a loved one die in spite of fervent prayer, and questioned God's power or very existence. You may have seen 'faith healers' who've manipulated the vulnerable and taken money for themselves, leaving a temporary euphoria followed by profound disappointment and frustration.

Other readers, however, may have encountered people with humility, common sense and a gift of healing which they place at God's disposal. Perhaps you have witnessed changes in the people for whom they have prayed – sometimes even changes that defy medical knowledge or human understanding – and have attributed that restoration to the power of prayer, the grace of God.

So maybe your answer to the question 'Does God *still* heal?' is 'sometimes' or 'yes and no' as, teetering on the uncomfortable edge of mystery, you face the reality that some prayers for healing seem to be answered and others ignored.[15]

---

15 For a readable, comprehensive treatment of this dilemma, see Philip Yancey, *Prayer: Does it Make any Difference?* Zondervan, 2006.

Part of our frustration with God's apparent 'lack of response' may lie in the narrowness of our vision, our culturally determined fixation with the 'quick fix' and *cure* as opposed to *healing*, and our focus on the *physical* to the exclusion of the emotional, relational and spiritual needs of the person for whom we pray. Jesus was focused on healing the *whole* person; he was concerned not just to restore functionality in the deaf, blind and the lame, but to strengthen personhood and reconnect them with their community. If we look at Jesus, our understanding of what constitutes healing is broadened so the person's *whole* life is considered, with *all* its elements, not just the physical.

The western cult of the individual would have us believe that fulfilment and wholeness can be attained through one's own efforts. But it is only through our interactions with others in the midst of ordinary life that we come to understand our frail and fractured selves and our need of God and community. Consequently, healing takes many forms. I think of a family reunited around their dying mother, past failures of communication healed by long silent hugs, by honesty and tears and forgiveness and the sharing of memories as blood-ties were reclaimed. I think of my own mum, whose childhood experience of rejection and a lifetime of melancholy was redeemed by persistent neighbourly love and a welcoming community. I think too of someone who had been estranged from the church for decades but who wanted to find his way back to faith in a way that made sense to him. We talked about the ministry of reconciliation – the opportunity, in private, to make a confession, and to hear pronounced the ancient words of absolution. As priest and as penitent, we placed ourselves in the stream of God's healing love and marvelled at how the Spirit met him, uniquely, beautifully, powerfully. Later, at peace, he rejoined the faith community and made his first communion since his wife's untimely death over 20 years ago.

I think too of an old lady, whom I shall call Ruth, who made a great effort to come to a retreat in daily life. In the daily, half-hour sessions, I listened to her never-before-shared story of childhood abuse and her lifetime burdens of grief, anger and shame. Halfway through the retreat, Ruth came to see me with her face shining: one of the resources, a particular poem, had engaged her in her time of prayer. She told me that, as she read and sat with and read aloud and prayed and read yet again, she found herself in conversation with the central character, Christ, and knew herself to be accepted, heard and healed. As Ruth read the poem aloud to me, my eyes filled with tears. I had never heard it read with such grace and power and truth. I knew that she had encountered the Living One who had touched her soul and spirit in the most gentle and appropriate way. And the poem? It was George Herbert's 'Love bade me welcome' – an invitation from Christ to sit and eat, to be his guest and delight. Ruth had indeed found herself the welcomed guest.

Within the church there is a strong tradition of healing ministry, expressed not by the more flamboyant 'faith healers' but in the steady prayers of intercession uttered week in and week out, in the laying on of hands and the sacraments of reconciliation and anointing with holy oil, and in the context of friendship, forgiveness, listening, acceptance and affirmation in which we can all play our part.

People are not healed in isolation. The community of faith is at the heart of healing; the warmth of our welcome and common life matters to the recovering alcoholic, to the solo parent who has staggered away from a violent relationship, to the aging priest whose illness prevents her from celebrating the Eucharist.

We see this truth played out in the story of the man who seeks healing at the pools at Bethesda because of his physical disability, the impact of which had clearly affected his sense of connection to his community. He is apparently alone, with no one to support or care for him. Perhaps his illness has so consumed his life and turned him inwards, that compassion has dried up, helpful neighbours or extended family have faded into the background and he is left to his own devices, lying there at Bethesda in one of the porticoes, in the hope of finding healing – somehow.

We are not told in this passage of others who did find healing there, only of the man who had waited and been disappointed for so many years – someone else always got there first, someone else always got touched by God, someone else always found friends to help them. Someone else ... but not him.

Someone else ... but not you? Is disappointment part of your story too? Are you longing for healing of something that has troubled you for a very long time? Are you hoping for some sort of miraculous intervention which will lift you up from your place of despair into the strong arms of Jesus, who will ask you that searingly simple question: 'Do you want to be made well?'

Jesus asked the man at Bethesda that question and asks us today:

א Are you willing to let go of the way you have seen yourself over these years as victim, as powerless, as isolated from others?
א Are you willing to take your share of responsibility as a fully contributing member of your community?
א Are you ready to take up the life Jesus offers with all its challenges and freedom?

I was 61 when I came to the pools at Bethesda. A group of us were attending a course at St George's Theological College in Jerusalem and had been considering Jesus as Healer. We were freshly awed by the stories of his miraculous touch, his gentle and generous giving of himself to so many, his reaching out to those who were on the margins, but also to those in power who recognized their need of grace, of God. And now, as we were given time to wander around the Bethesda ruins, the very site of the healing described in the Gospel passage with which you have just prayed, I was even more struck by this reality.

As I looked at the ruins and then sat and allowed my mind to become receptive to the movement of the Spirit, several thoughts came and went. Nothing seemed to need attention until, in simple silent words, a Spirit-gift suggestion formed: 'seek healing for the shame of your fatherlessness'. I was stunned – I had never known the identity of my father, but for the last three decades God had been gently guiding me through the hurts of the past, healing my grief, helping me express my anger at his absence from my life, bringing me through to a place of acceptance and peace. But, clearly, God thought there was still some work to do and had brought me to this moment with exquisite timing and provision.

Shame is the most fundamental of all hurts, for shame strikes at the heart of who we are, not what we do. And so it was that, in this holy place thousands of miles from my home, I went for prayer to the St George's chaplain, who at that time just 'happened' to be a woman priest from my own diocese whom I knew and trusted. Touched by my friend's tender presence and prayerful wisdom, I received the gift of release from that unspoken sense of inadequacy that had stunted my soul. Later that same afternoon, gentle words of assurance formed in my mind, as if Jesus himself were speaking: 'Now I bear that wound for you.'

Does God still heal? I would have to say 'yes'. Absolutely, yes!

Yes. Unexpectedly, not always as we might imagine, not always to cure physical illness, but seeking to help us be free to live and love fully, and to be bearers of God's grace to others. Jesus is willing to bear our wounds for us if we are willing to name them and bring them to his compassionate heart. Will you do that today?

Deepening

✠ If what has been written above touches a chord in you, spend some time quietly in prayer, listening for the particular way forward that God has shaped just for you.
Don't worry if it is not immediately apparent – when the time is right, an opportunity will arise which will bring you towards wholeness.

✠ How have you seen the healing love and power of God at work in those around you or for whom you pray?

✠ What wound would you like Jesus to bear for you today?

✠ If there have been frustrations and disappointments related to the question of healing in the past, bring these to God as honestly as you can, even if you are angry or disbelieving or doubtful – tell it 'like it is'.

Closing prayer

God of all our days,
you hold us in our unknowing
as we grapple with the mystery
of life and death and healing.
Be with us as we deconstruct
our walls of certainty
and give your
Spirit room to
enter our inner pain.
Soothe our anguish,
salve our anxiety,
wrap us round
with the love of Christ,
that we may be held
close to the heart of God
where healing happens ...
and hope flies free once more.
AMEN

On holiday with God

On the mountain top – *choosing to listen*

Focus verse

O that my people would listen to me,
that Israel would walk in my ways!
(Psalm 81.13)

Opening prayer

Lord,
I am not deaf,
but still I struggle to hear your voice
in the clamour of the common chaos,
swirling round my ears.
You are not in the whirlwind,
nor in the storm or earthquake,
but in the stillness
of my soul,
as I rest and as I move
through the day's demands,
if I have heart to hear.
Teach me to tend a listening space
within my busy being,
that your timely teaching
may reach my core
and strengthen me
for service.
AMEN

Scripture to use for lectio divina *or imaginative prayer*

²Six days later, Jesus took with him Peter and James and John,
and led them up a high mountain apart, by themselves. And he
was transfigured before them, ³and his clothes became dazzling
white, such as no one on earth could bleach them. ⁴And there
appeared to them Elijah with Moses, who were talking with Jesus.

⁵Then Peter said to Jesus, 'Rabbi, it is good for us to be here; let us make three dwellings, one for you, one for Moses, and one for Elijah.' ⁶He did not know what to say, for they were terrified. ⁷Then a cloud overshadowed them, and from the cloud there came a voice, 'This is my Son, the Beloved; listen to him!' ⁸Suddenly when they looked around, they saw no one with them any more, but only Jesus.

⁹As they were coming down the mountain, he ordered them to tell no one about what they had seen, until after the Son of Man had risen from the dead.

(Mark 9.2–9)

Personal reflection

៩ What thoughts and feelings surface as you immerse yourself in this dramatic story?

៩ Have you ever had a religious or spiritual experience which has taken you by surprise? What happened?
With whom have you shared that moment?

៩ 'The fear of the LORD is the beginning of wisdom ...'
(Psalm 111.10a).

How does this verse relate to the passage before you today and to your own journey of faith?

Further food for thought

Time apart with their beloved teacher – what a gift for these three faithful disciples! As they trudged up the mountain, I wonder what was going through their minds? Were they looking forward to some deeper, personal teaching, or a planning session on how to build the Kingdom of God? Perhaps they longed for answers to questions simmering in the background of their minds. Whatever they were hoping for, they certainly weren't expecting a super-natural encounter with Moses and Elijah, the embodiment of the Law and the Prophets, emerging from eternity to flank the One who was the fulfilment of them both. Nor were they anything like prepared to see their down-to-earth and dusty Master, lit from within by the incandescent Spirit of God.

No wonder they were terrified! No wonder Peter in his characteristic extraversion blurts out the first words that come into his head, suggesting that they capture the moment by building booths for each of the three shimmering figures. And then, as if there were not already enough wonder to last a lifetime, mystery wraps them round in a misty blanket, and a voice is heard:

THIS IS MY SON, THE BELOVED. *LISTEN* TO HIM!

Listen to him, to Jesus, God tells them, and tells us still today. For millennia God has offered human beings covenant relationship, the invitation to live in heart-to-heart communion with the Trinity as beloved adult children of God. Yet repeatedly, wilfully, there is a sorry pattern of disobedience on an individual and a community level. In the Old Testament we see kings come to power who intend to rule according to God's laws, but few manage to leave successors who will follow their example. Over and over again, Israel goes after 'other gods' and turns its back on the true God who cares for them so much, as the psalmist writes, giving expression to God's yearning for relationship:

> Hear, O my people, while I admonish you;
> O Israel, if you would but listen to me!
> There shall be no strange god among you;
> you shall not bow down to a foreign god.
> I am the LORD your God,
> who brought you up out of the land of Egypt.
> Open your mouth wide and I will fill it.
> But my people did not listen to my voice;
> Israel would not submit to me.
> So I gave them over to their stubborn hearts ...
> (Psalm 81.8–12a)

Israel's rebellion and deafness to God's teaching and loving inevitably leads to defeat and despair, yet God still longs to fight Israel's battles and provide the best for his chosen people. Then and now, God is both understanding of human weakness and frustrated by human stubbornness. Perhaps that is why God chooses to tell the stunned disciples witnessing the transfiguration to *listen*. God could have reminded them about the needs of the poor and the widow, or encouraged them to keep focused on sharing the good news in ever widening ripples of hope. Instead God let them know that the *most important* thing they, and anyone, can do is to listen to Jesus – to the voice of the Son whose life, death and resurrection provide hope and healing for humanity.

Some of us are not naturally good listeners in a human context, let alone in listening to God. We might be distracted by our busyness, racing ahead to form answers or darting around seeking ways to fix things, instead of simply *being with* another person, trying to see things from their perspective, trying to hear the emotion behind the words. If this is how we act with people, then the risk is that we shall also find listening to God difficult: our prayer will likely consist of telling God what we think God ought to do, or talking to God all the time instead of stopping to listen. If you fall into this category, then bring to God your desire to learn to listen. Begin to notice your listening capacity or lack of it, and then ask for the grace you need to respond to Jesus when he says:

Come to me, all you that are weary and carrying heavy
burdens, and I will give you rest.
Take my yoke upon you and *learn from me*;
for I am gentle and humble in heart,
and you will find rest for your souls.
For my yoke is easy, and my burden is light.
(Matthew 11.28–30, my emphasis)

Some of us choose *not* to listen. We unconsciously, or even deliberately, avoid intimacy with others and with God; some of us are fearful that if we get too close, if we reveal too much of ourselves, we will give the other party too much influence in our lives; we will lose that illusion of control which human beings covet. Others of us are weak and wilful; we really don't want to listen to what God is saying to us because we don't intend to obey.

If you recognize this avoidance or contrariness in your nature, be assured that it is not beyond God's forgiveness. Take this shadow aspect of yourself and lay it at the foot of the cross in prayer so you can be freed from its power, freed to hear your Lord's words to you. God knows this dynamic in us and still speaks the message of peace and freedom: a message which Jesus came to declare, calling from a cross erected roughly in a quarry outside the walls of Jerusalem two thousand years ago.

So how does God 'speak' to us? What are we listening for?

Traditionally God speaks to us in our inner world through the Holy Spirit who, using our marvellous mind, prompts us to action, brings new insights, reminds us of precious words of Scripture, alerts us to need in others, suggests creative responses to awkward situations, brings helpful dreams at times of key decision-making or crisis, releases tears as we sense God's presence or healing touch ...

But the voice of God can also come to us in our outer world. Sometimes God 'speaks' through the words of others, through acts of compassion and care, through the beauty of creation, through the gaze of a child, through the timing of events whether we call them 'God-incidences' or 'synchronicity', through one opportunity opening up while another closes, through singing and Scripture spoken and broken open, through music and birdsong, through artworks and literature ...

You can see how important it is that we learn to listen to the whole of our life. Wherever you are and whatever you are doing, God can meet you at any point and bring what you need for that moment. Your role in this holy alliance is to tend a listening space in your soul, a place of quiet receptivity even in the midst of the tasks and toil of everyday life, so that you *can hear* God's voice and be guided by the Spirit in every undertaking.

How do you tend this listening space?

✠ By trusting that God is already at work in you
✠ by giving your assent to Spirit-led growth
✠ by taking time to reflect on your daily experience through keeping a spiritual journal and the practice of the examen
✠ by cherishing moments of intentional solitude and silence

✠ by learning from little children as they slowly explore the world with fresh eyes and model the practice of contemplation
✠ by praying with Scripture to refresh your spirit and build up a storehouse of God's word within you
✠ by spending time out of doors, enjoying the beauty of creation
✠ by reducing noise and clutter
✠ by soothing your spirit with music that sings to you of God
✠ by recognizing the presence of God in every struggle of suffering, in every act of love.

Over time this listening space within you will grow, and you will find yourself drawn to a form of prayer in which you say very little, just a simple anchor phrase or word that helps your mind stay centred on God. You 'turn up' as it were, and sit with God, as you might sit with your best friend or spouse, happy in each others' company without need of conversation. What is different though is that in this time of companionable silence, God's Spirit is working directly with your spirit, dismantling well-established ego defences that are ready to be relinquished, bringing intimations of healing, strengthening you for service and helping you *know* deep within that you are, as God names his own son in this transfiguration passage, *beloved. Knowing* this settles your spirit, soothes your soul, warms your heart and enables your mission. For this is the bottom line: God loves you, God loves me, now and forever, no matter what:

> For I am convinced that neither death, nor life,
> nor angels, nor rulers, nor things present, nor
> things to come, nor powers, nor height, nor depth,
> nor anything else in all creation, will be able to
> separate us from the love of God in Christ Jesus our LORD.
> (Romans 8.38–39)

Peter's rushed attempt to capture the moment – a bit like a tourist taking out his digital device and snapping a segment of experience to share with folks back home – is symptomatic of our fear of losing the wonder of something that transcends normal life. We can even think that, after a heart-stopping spiritual experience, we shall never again feel God's touch or tenderness, that we've had our 'ration' of divine encounter and we'd better hang on to it with both hands, in case this is the one and only time God will connect with us. But nothing could be further from the truth. While the transfiguration was an amazing experience for Peter, we know from the Acts of the Apostles that God continued to meet Peter in ways that were timely and vivid, giving him what he needed when he needed it, not always spectacularly but always appropriately.

God is there for you too, not just in the surprising moments of insight, answered prayer, synchronicity or 'God-incidences', or felt awareness of the divine Presence, but also in the midst of everyday life – if you are listening. And who wouldn't want to listen when, with your listening space available to God, any time you need to ask for wisdom, even in the middle of a difficult situation, you have only to take a moment to share your reality with the eternal Reality, trusting that the way forward will be given, the words will be available when you need them. This is on one level nerve-wracking, on another level energizing: trusting God for what you need as you need it, moment by moment, happens as you do your prayerful preparation, are willing to be guided by the Spirit of God, and as you open yourself to the needs of those around you in loving service.

- The more you listen to Jesus, the calmer your centre, no matter what storms rage about you.
- The more you listen to Jesus, the more open to the invitation of the Spirit you become.
- The more you listen to Jesus, the more courageous your living, the more likely you will be able to follow Jesus wherever he leads you.

Deepening

- How have you heard God 'speak' to you in your inner world of mind, will and emotion, or in your outer world of circumstances and synchronicity or 'God-moments'?

On the mountain top – choosing to listen

✠ Consider your circumstances and then prayerfully review the Romans passage above, being open to how God might want to meet you in the details of your life.

✠ Re-read what I said on 'tending your listening space' on pages 133–4. How does this relate to your current spiritual practices? You may want to consider times when you have or have not heard clearly from God and what that meant to you and those around you.

✠ When you have had time to think, pray about your desire to keep a space open into which the Spirit may speak …

Closing prayer

Jesus, you listen to the pain
of the world
and weep at our rebellion,
knowing that all we have to do
is turn to you, to be healed.
Lord, I want to turn to you.
I want to listen to your love,
to your life and example
of self-giving commitment
to those who are in need.
I want to listen to my life too,
to hear your wisdom echoing
through the common things,
to tune in to the sacred song
humming through each day,
to discover how I can be
an agent of your grace,
in spite of my shortcomings.
For that is your call to me,
to share in your kingdom life
and bring life to others
in your name.
AMEN

6

Closing liturgy and prayer: Gathering the gifts of the retreat

Choose from the following elements and shape this prayer time to reflect the content and process of the retreat. Use your own prayers.

Setting up your prayer space for this final time.

Lighting the 'Christ' candle.

Music.

Reviewing the retreat – remembering high points and struggles, meaning and memories, questions and discoveries.

Placing of symbol/s to represent significant moment/s.

Reading – Scripture, poetry or portions of your spiritual journal.

Silence.

Thanksgiving.

Singing.

Offering to God your hopes for the future.

Acknowledging the ending of this retreat time by slowly removing the items from the prayer space.

On Holiday with God

Extinguishing the 'Christ' candle with the words:

Light of Christ, continue to shine in me
as I leave this place and return home.
Jesus, may I be your voice and hands
with my family and in my community;
may I draw daily on the grace and guidance of the
Holy Spirit and walk with the joy of God in my heart.
AMEN

7

Home-going and continuing on 'The Way'

Understandably, Peter didn't want that mystical moment of trans-figuration on the mountain top (Mark 9.2–10), to end, so he suggested building a shelter to be a visible reminder of the mystery they had witnessed. But that idea and the moment didn't last, the shimmering figures of Moses and Elijah disappeared, and Jesus was 'back to normal' as far as they could see. They all had to 'come down off the mountain' and, as you come to the end of your retreat time, so do you.

Like Peter, you may not want to leave a place where you have experienced some graced encounters with God. Perhaps you are reluctant to get back into the maelstrom of life at home. Perhaps you even feel a bit anxious about whether what has been gifted to you on retreat will remain accessible when you resume 'normal life'. But there is no need to be afraid, because in a beautiful way, you are not entirely the same person who came on holiday with God a short while ago. Even if nothing 'spectacular' has hap-pened, you have spent dedicated time with the Holy One, and will forever carry with you the fragrance of God's love for you.

When you have planned your closing liturgy and prayed your farewell, if you have enough time, pack up after your retreat *slowly*, letting yourself quietly take leave of the place and any areas that have acquired special meaning for you. If you are driv-ing home, be aware that you may have slowed down so much while on holiday with God that the fast pace of the traffic may take you by surprise!

Use the bulk of the return journey as an opportunity to reflect and enjoy some of the moments of grace experienced over the

time you have been away. Then, as you get closer to home, begin to turn your mind and prayer to what awaits you. Bring these things and people to God, one by one, and know that God hears you and will answer in the way that is best for you and those you love. You do not return home alone, but with the knowledge that God is with you, closer than breathing, only a thought away.

And what do you say when you get home? How much do you share? After all, following the wonder of the transfiguration, Jesus clearly told his disciples to keep quiet about their experience:

As they were coming down the mountain,
he ordered them to tell no one about what
they had seen, until after the Son of Man had
risen from the dead.
(Mark 9.10)

This seems a difficult instruction; after what the disciples had seen, they would naturally want to tell others about the amazing spiritual experience and glorious insight they had into the nature of Jesus and his relationship with the Father. But Jesus was absolutely clear: there was to be no sharing of this experience until resurrection was a reality.

It's natural for you to want to share what you have discovered too, so does Jesus' caution have any relevance for you, now? Consider this question: have you ever told someone something very precious to you, only to have them respond in a way that diminished your story, leaving you wishing you had said nothing, or feeling as if what you had said was foolish? If you have, then you understand something of what Jesus was thinking when he warned his disciples, and you will recognize the value of discretion when considering how much to share with other people.

What Jesus advises his disciples rings true for any of us who have had a special moment with God. They were told to wait until after the resurrection, until the time when the Spirit of God would be free to enliven and guide every person who sought God's indwelling and needed to discern God's truth. The Spirit of God is available to all believers, so *you* can be guided by the Spirit when discerning who might be able to appreciate what has been significant for you during your retreat. Such a person needs to be a respectful listener, an open-minded man or woman of faith, someone whose maturity you value, whose confidentiality you trust, and who knows about your genuine longing for God.

If you have no one with whom to share your God-stories, then continue to keep your spiritual journal, and begin to look for a spiritual director or soul friend, someone who knows the dynamics of the life of faith and is able to offer you companionship on the way. Incidentally, the word 'director' here doesn't mean he or she will tell you what to do. Rather it relates to their commitment to helping you maintain *your* spiritual direction, supporting *your* journey with God.

Often people find a suitable spiritual director via word of mouth, so you might like to begin by asking people whom you think might understand what you are looking for or contacting a local diocesan office. Another option would be to visit the websites of organizations offering spiritual direction or retreat ministry, for example:

In the United Kingdom: www.retreats.org.uk
In Australia: www.ansd.org.au
In New Zealand: www.acsd.org.nz or www.sgm.org.nz
In North America and other countries: www.sdiworld.org

All of the above websites can also put you in touch with other retreat opportunities and locations in case you want to start planning your next holiday with God right away!

You and God have taken a unique holiday together during this retreat time. Whether you have practised praying with Scripture, or you have noticed common things that have the capacity to speak to you of God; whether you have begun to see and believe that you are beloved of God and so are other people; or whether you have taken time at night to think about your day and see what has drawn you closer to God...

Whatever you and God have been up to on this retreat, your

view of yourself, your family, your community, and your God may well have changed. Because you now know that the *whole* of life can speak of the presence of God when you listen, when you stop long enough to see. The distinction between sacred and secular has dissolved and you know more of the reality of God 'in whom we live and move and have our being' (Acts 17.28).

When you return home and pick up the routines and responsibilities that await you, you may wonder what comes next in your faith journey. You may wonder how to cherish the softened spirit within you, how to hold on to the hints of healing, how to explore the new questions, how to express the deepening sense of love or compassion, or how to give thanks for the grace experienced during this holiday with God. The good news is that this is God's responsibility, and God's work with you on this retreat will continue as long as you want to stay on the journey. As the apostle Paul wrote:

> I am confident of this, that the one who began a good work among you will bring it to completion by the day of Jesus Christ. (Philippians 1.6)

The Holy Spirit will guide you and help you give priority to your faith journey as you begin to incorporate simple spiritual disciplines into your day:

> If you begin each day with a few minutes with God, naming your concerns, asking for the grace you need, and the awareness to notice God in the midst of the everyday, you will be well on the way towards keeping the light of Christ alive in you.

> Somewhere during your day, take a few verses of a Gospel and mull them over, letting something emerge which touches your soul, make your prayer response and then sit quietly with God for a while – and thus a simple *lectio divina* practice begins.

> Similarly, if at day's end you spend a few minutes reviewing the events and emotions of the day, making a note in your spiritual journal about when you have drawn closer to God or what

has taken you further away, you will be building up an understanding of what God is doing in your life, where the areas of challenge are, where the new life is emerging.

You are on a journey of discovery to explore the 'more' of God. At times this journey will be awe-inspiring, frustrating, delightful, poignant, challenging, gentle, a roller-coaster, consoling – and never dull!

God loves you and wants you to reach your potential, to bear God's image brightly in the world and do what no other person can do – be fully yourself. That is your gift to God.

You are not alone, as Jesus says (Matthew 28.20b):

And remember, I am with you always,
to the end of the age.

May the God of grace bless you and continue to strengthen you for this journey.

AMEN.